Herbert Martin

A girl's past

Vol. I

Herbert Martin

A girl's past
Vol. I

ISBN/EAN: 9783337051006

Printed in Europe, USA, Canada, Australia, Japan

Cover: Foto ©ninafisch / pixelio.de

More available books at **www.hansebooks.com**

A GIRL'S PAST

A NOVEL

BY

Mrs HERBERT MARTIN

AUTHOR OF 'BONNIE LESLEY,' 'COMMON CLAY,'
'A MAN AND A BROTHER,' ETC., ETC.

IN THREE VOLUMES

VOL. I.

LONDON
F. V. WHITE & CO.
31 SOUTHAMPTON STREET, STRAND, W.C.

1893

All Rights reserved.

A maid whom there were none to praise,
And very few to love.

	PAGE
CHAPTER I.	1
CHAPTER II.	20
CHAPTER III.	45
CHAPTER IV.	64
CHAPTER V.	86
CHAPTER VI.	114
CHAPTER VII.	139
CHAPTER VIII.	170
CHAPTER IX.	199
CHAPTER X.	214
CHAPTER XI.	239

A GIRL'S PAST

A GIRL'S PAST.

CHAPTER I.

'THEN you are really going down to take possession of your property, to-morrow, Monsieur le Prince? Don't you feel big? I really wonder we see no difference in you!'

Graham Brooke-Graham looked up from the beloved old gun he was cleaning, and smiled at his small, lively, brunette sister, who perched herself on the table of his smoking-room, and glanced him over with her rather small but brightly brown eyes. Mrs Brooke, who had come in to rummage in a cupboard for something necessary for the packing which busied her at present, looked a little grave at her daughter's levity. Mrs Brooke was an excellent woman, with a supreme regard for the fitting. Of course it was a great blessing, an enormous relief, to a widow of small means, that her only son's distant cousin and godfather, John Graham of Erdley, should have taken so great a fancy to his namesake as to make him his heir, and then leave the world while that heir was only eight-and-twenty; but it is not *comme il faut* to rejoice too openly at the results of a death, which should always modify the tones and sadden the countenance.

'Kitty, dear,' she said in faint remonstrance, 'it is hardly fitting; Graham was fond of his cousin, he is only lately dead.'

'Oh! I know he liked the poor old man. I know he did not wish him gone; but since he *is* gone, mater, and human nature *is* human nature, Graham may be allowed to enjoy the idea of his princeship.'

'I was happy enough before,' Graham said slowly; then, in deference to the impatient protest of Kitty's shoulders against humbug, he added, 'but I don't pretend to be above being glad to have Erdley. They say the shooting is jolly good this year.'

A month ago, Graham Brooke-Graham (with a *hyphen*) had been simple Graham Brooke, of the Military Store Department of the War Office; now he was a landed proprietor, possessing a rent-roll of some thousands—by no means a millionaire, but grandly promoted, in the eyes of a mother and sister used to the modest and thrifty ways of a small establishment at Putney. Mrs Graham felt, somehow, as if she were personally to be praised for the result—for bringing so successful, so delightful a son into the world. There was, she believed, an immense deal both in heredity and education. Graham had good blood in him, and no one could justly say she had ever spoiled her only son. She greatly plumed herself on him, as she did on Kitty's social success at balls, where she always danced as much and had as many admirers as far more handsome girls. The brother and sister were not in the least alike: Kitty, as we have said, was small, dark, vivacious; Graham had a fair skin, before foreign service (for he had been both in Africa and India) had tanned him to a rich mahogany; his short-cropped hair was light brown, his eyes calm, steadfast, persistent grey. He was not handsome; his nose left much to be desired, and he had no really beautiful traits; but his rather large, close-shut mouth had a sweet expression, and his round, firm chin, a somewhat attractive dimple. He was not very tall, but broad-shouldered, well-proportioned, with an air of easy strength. The most undemonstrative of men, he was yet always liked by men and women; one of the least eloquent and showy, yet no one ever thought him stupid, he had an oddly penetrating habit of understanding things and people—children were fond of him, animals adored him, girls trusted him. He was of a purely English type; but the ordinary John-Bullish obstinacy of prejudice one might have expected to find with this physique had been somehow turned into tolerance by a pretty extensive acquaintance with other countries and peoples. Enough of description! It is very likely nine people out of ten would not have looked at Brooke-Graham twice, yet he was not insignificant or contemptible for all that. He had been in the habit of visiting Mr Graham of Erdley whenever he could spare time; but, as it happened, he had been two years at the Cape, from which he only returned some weeks before his cousin's sudden death; so he had not been there for some time, and had not shot over the Erdley preserves for four seasons. Graham was a keen sportsman, and was looking forward to the pheasant-shooting of the month on which he was just entering. He went down to Gloucestershire the following day, and this was the 29th of September. He was going alone— partly because his most intimate chums were scattered, partly because Erdley wanted a good deal doing to it to make it a really agreeable place to stay in, even for bachelors. Mr Graham had been much of a recluse — a bookish, low-spirited man, who cared little for social life. He had buried himself in an untidy library, allowed two or three old servants to cheat him at their pleasure, and had given up in despair attempting to put anything right in a world which he felt to be hopelessly tangled and chaotic. 'Oh, yes! I know, I know!' he would cry, wringing his delicate hands, when the Rector insisted on explaining to him how sad and bad everything in the village was, and how sorely in need of reform. 'My dear sir, I know it all! English social life is rotten to the core—from the highest to the lowest stratum, corruption is slowly penetrating. Will twenty pounds help you out at all?'

And Mr Merryweather, the Rector, generally found that it *would*. The new young Squire of Erdley meant, in his silent heart, to do very differently from his predecessor. He would let sunshine and air through the house; would give away a lot of the books; he was no dullard, and liked reading well enough, but he liked the life of every day, open air, men and women, much better. He would shoot over the neglected preserves, furnish the dingy rooms, mix freely in the doings and socialities of the place, make himself acquainted with the habits and customs of the country folks. He had no pride in him, not an idea of starting on a higher level than his neighbours; he had many and practical schemes of goodwill. Then — in time—when things were straight and the manor-house as he liked it, he would take home some nice, 'jolly,' clever girl, and lead a wholesome, happy, country life—keeping himself from getting rusty by occasional flights to town, to Paris, or further afield. Life looked calmly radiant in Brooke-Graham's eyes as he whistled like a lark over his gun-cleaning, and made arrangements for his visit to his lately-acquired property.

'A man in your position, dear, ought to have a *valet*,' his mother said, suddenly appearing at his door with another dozen of handkerchiefs fresh from the laundress.

'A *what?*' he asked absently, stopping his whistle and staring at her.

'A valet — a man-servant,' she repeated, faltering a little, however, as she saw the smile dawn on his shut mouth, and twinkle in his honest grey eyes. 'I know you are very independent and democratic in your ideas; but, really, dear, I think you *ought*.'

'What do you suppose will happen if I don't?'

'Oh! nothing; only, it may seem singular. Mr Calbraith has, and he is not in so good a position as you are now.'

'No, mater; I don't think I'll indulge in a valet. Old Rogers, my cousin's factotum, isn't a bad sort; he can fill my bath, and so on, when I want anything. I don't relish the idea of a fine gentleman overhauling my shirts and sneering at my rough-and-ready ways. I prefer to spend the money on a nice maid for you and Kit; she said she would like one who could make up frocks and hats for her. You know I sha'n't be so enormously rich when all's said and done.'

'But you're too generous, Graham. You want to spend too much on Kitty and me. We are quite comfortable as we are.'

'Ay,' he returned, smiling. 'I know

all your little dodges, mater; don't try and take me in. I've heard you settling to have "high tea" (of all abominations), instead of a proper dinner, because I was going out; and, I know, one day Kitty declared she hadn't had lunch enough, and felt as hungry as when she sat down.'

'That was only Kitty's nonsense,' the mother cried, a little vexed at the exposure of her small economies. 'It is ridiculous to have a great spread for two women.'

'That's women's way. But I choose you should have as big a spread as you like. You want to make a selfish brute of me.'

'No, dearest; I could not do that.'

'Well,' he returned, getting up and stretching himself, with the clean, polished gun, held out at length in one hand, 'at any rate, you will do your best to try.'

'It was always Kitty, not you, who was the selfish one, from childhood,' she persisted, gazing fondly at him.

He frowned a little. It now and then annoyed him to witness her unwavering partiality; but it never vexed Kitty, who took life on the surface, with happy ease.

'I don't think that's quite fair on Kit. She *cared* for things more than I did, that's all. She's not selfish; and as for me, I'm quite as capable of grabbing and sticking to what I want as any one, only it doesn't occur to me to want things very badly as a rule.'

He packed his gun carefully into its case, in the deliberate, methodical, orderly way he had, with dexterous fingers, then sat down to fill and light his shabby, old pipe, which he never would exchange for the expensive meerschaums which had from time to time been presented to him. Graham had a curious, pertinacious constancy in all his tastes and habits; he never lost a friend nor gave up a custom, if he could help it. As he puffed slowly through his first pipe—which took him a long time—he revolved his past, present and future in his calm exhaustive fashion. He was no facile talker, and had little skill in clothing thought in eloquence; yet he thought much, and had dreams, ideals, hopes and speculations which, if put into words, would a good deal have surprised even his intimates. He had been through some adventures, had faced death more than once; in a skirmish in Africa; at sea; in an attack of fever — these things had left their traces on a mind naturally retentive and persistent. In that fever, when he was delirious, he had surprised the friend that nursed him by revealing odd depths and powers, strange revelations of unimagined secrets in a state of half delirium. It had cured that friend of thinking him as only a 'good old chap,' a 'decent fellow, with nothing very remarkable in him, you know.' Ever after he declared there was more under Brooke's quiet skin than any one knew. But Brooke had a great power of 'keeping himself to himself,' as the servants say.

'I daresay,' he was thinking, as he slowly let out clouds of smoke, 'things aren't going to be at all what I map out; there's no accounting for the vagaries of life. It seems all smooth sailing now, but I shall very likely get among some breakers after a bit. I *mean* to be jolly happy, and have a right easy time of it, but fortune may mean just differently. The poor old man didn't enjoy his life there much; it's true he was not, like me—much more thin-skinned, more of a pessimist, the sort much thinking makes lean or mad. I sha'n't go his way to work, I'll keep my eyes open and my ears, and see if there's anything very particular wanting to be done. Not the old beef, coal-and-blanket work of bygone days. Squire and Lady Bountiful, smiling dames in red cloaks, innocent peasant beauties, and all the past stock-in-trade that's played out; it's a day of school boards and county councils now, of strikes and allotments. I must be up to the spirit of the time. I wish there were a more modern specimen at the Rectory than old Merryweather. He's not bad, but quite an anachronism; he sees there are sores, and he sets to work with his ancient plasters and nostrums that don't do a bit of good. Church is his one idea of saving the souls of the poor folks—unrelenting, undeviating, unattractive church services; beef-tea and blue pills are his remedies for the suffering bodies. They get what they can out of the poor old boy, and laugh at him at home. I won't be blarneyed to my face, and scoffed at behind my back.

I'll get at the people, and clear off the humbug. There's some grit under it when one can reach it. Poor old Graham never could. He shrank from the poor people, their coarse talk, their ugliness, their old clothes, their soft sawder when they wanted anything, their abuse when they couldn't get it. I won't shrink. I won't expect the impossible, and we shall see.' So the day of Brooke-Graham's entry on his small kingdom began — in smoke.

The fair September weather—fair and blue to its last hour — smiled serenely over the red brick house at Erdley; the garden, woods and fallow fields, the brooding hills and green sloping meadow of the country place, that seemed also to smile, waiting, as autumn lingered, for its coming master. Graham Brooke-Graham had truly come into a 'goodly heritage.' To-morrow would see him in possession of it.

CHAPTER II.

THE following, morning Mr Brooke-Graham, his well-worn portmanteau, gun-case and bag, were conveyed to the London station in due time for the train for Oldfield Junction and Erdley. As he followed in line before the ticket office, he was rather amused to hear a suave, distinct, unmistakably clerical accent, demanding—'Four and a half for Erdley, if you please;' then equally distinctly—'by the way, could you kindly inform me *where* I change for Erdley? There seems some little confusion—'

Graham looked at the speaker in some surprise at finding any one beside himself *en route* for so small and remote a place, but he had lived long enough to understand how small the world is. It was a shortish man, with a rather rusty clergyman's soft hat on his head, wearing a sort of cloak of an equally seedy appearance; grey locks that had not long before been light, which seemed to need a good deal of brushing, rested on the collar of this garment; the face, when turned in profile, was neat featured, rather red in complexion, with greyish whiskers and moustache, of an old-fashioned cut, somewhat *à la* Dundreary.

'No, sir,' the ticket clerk snapped back in return; 'it is not my business to give information about changes; they'll tell you at the train. Come, sir, look sharp, please — three seventeen six.'

The payment seemed a lengthy business, and the delay caused by the fumbling for an ancient purse, the extraction of a black kid glove which looked as if it had done duty at countless funerals, and the slow searching, which eventually produced a crumpled five-pound note, made the most backward of the file of would-be travellers fidget and fume. At last the change was given and counted, the tickets grasped, and Graham could get his. On the departure platform, in front of the nearly empty train, he found the same clergyman inquiring anxiously of various impossible people where he was to change for Erdley. Graham had a foolish predilection for helping lame dogs over stiles, and went

A Girl's Past.   23

up, raising his hat courteously to a small group, all well laden with packages, who hovered near, keeping guard over a pile of very shabby-looking luggage.

'Excuse me, sir,' he said, in his slow, gentle voice, which gave an impression of indolence, contradicted by his observant, keen glance, 'I am going to Erdley. I can satisfy you on that point; you have to change twice—at Stroud and at Oldfield Junction—only ten miles from Erdley. The train leaves Oldfield at 5.15; we get to Erdley a few minutes past six.'

'Thank you, sir, thank you a hundred times!' the other cried effusively; 'it seemed as if no one could give me the desired information—as if Erdley were at the other end of nowhere. I am much obliged to you,'

'Not at all. It is sometimes difficult, I know, to get trustworthy answers, and Erdley *is* rather remote.' Raising his hat again, he fell back and watched the clergyman repeating his words to the ladies of his party. In truth, Graham regarded these same ladies a little fixedly.

He was in the twenties, and two of them were very young and very pretty, yet in totally different styles. It was easy to guess at the relationship of the party —father, mother and three daughters; two grown up, and the third a small, frail-looking child with a crutch, apparently not more than ten years old. The mother was tall, thin, a little haggard-looking—in fact, almost gaunt—yet she was only middle-aged, probably very little over forty, and had certainly been once a handsome girl. She had the indescribable air of trouble; care, not age, had evidently worn her—probably a long hand-to-hand fight with that poverty which grinds soul and body into attenuation. Her abundant hair was still dark, soft and wavy, though threaded with grey; her large, sunken eyes must have once been beautiful, now they were only resignedly quiescent, dimmed by unjoyful experiences; her complexion was sallow and unhealthy-looking; but, judging by one of the girls who was much like her, it might have been once, as the daughter's was now, a clear, creamy pale—the very tint to set off deep, dark eyes and straight, fine brows. Every beauty was marred and spoilt in the mother by the ruthless hand of the hag Care. The once soft, curved mouth, made for slow, sweet smiles, was dragged out of shape, and drooped into unlovely lines; the cheeks had fallen in, and the bones showed prominent; the long, well-shaped throat had grown scraggy; the once graceful figure angular, with the tired stoop of one accustomed to carry burdens. Yet withal, it was a gentle and attractive face, which might have struck one as still handsome, if the least care as to becomingness or nicety of toilette had set it off to any advantage. There was no attempt at this; the lady had evidently given up her own appearance hopelessly; she was dressed with the dowdy, disorderly shabbiness which some people think appropriate to a journey. The girls, on the contrary, had evidently somewhat studied their looks. One of them—a very fair, pretty, alert-looking maiden—had dressed her light locks with care and skill; some coquettish little curls were carefully arranged under her small home-made cloth toque, and caressed the slender nape of a white neck. She looked up and down and about her with the lively restlessness of a bird; her complexion was pretty, and her grey-blue eyes bright. The other girl was a perfect contrast in every single particular—in colouring, expression, feature, style, She had dark, almost dusky, hair, coarse and naturally curly, raised high without any fringe, only with, as it were, a kind of halo of rough, loose hair; a very picturesque and becoming, yet evidently unstudied, coiffure. Her complexion was absolutely pale — a creamy, yellowish pale—the only touch of red being on the rather full, plaintive mouth — the mouth of a child. The round, soft chin had a pretty, babyish dimple, but the expression of the face was not infantile at all, though she looked remarkably young—it was sad, reserved, rather brooding. The great, heavy-lidded, darkly-fringed brown eyes that met Graham's for a moment had a depth of wistful melancholy in them that touched and disturbed him. He thought he had never seen any girl at all like this one. After her sadness, it was a relief to hear the fair sister's chatter and laugh, and to see that the father also looked somewhat jovial. The little girl —the lame one—had a pale, small face, with some expression of physical pain on it, and a pair of large, dark, eager eyes, anxious to take in every detail *en voyage*.

'Going to Erdley, bag and baggage; I wonder who they can be?' thought Graham, as he watched his luggage in and chose his carriage, 'hardly to stay with Merryweather—such a tribe.'

He had the boyish curiosity to glance at the labels on the pile of ungainly luggage. 'Rev. W. W. Lane, passenger to Erdley.' He thought of the two pretty sisters once or twice before they reached the first change. Here he saw them all again on the platform, the clergyman in a considerable state of fuss; he got his womankind and baggage together, and then darted off to the refreshment-room.

'Is he going to get tea for the lot?' thought Graham, as he followed him; 'there will barely be time, but they look as if they wanted it.'

No, such was evidently not the intention of the head of the family. He was rapidly drinking off a modicum of whisky and water.

'Ha,' thought Graham, 'hence that slightly rubicund nose of yours, my friend. Are you also one of the "nipping" sort? I feel rather sorry for Madame votre femme.'

Turning from the buffet, the clergyman encountered his friend-in-need, and smiled agreeably, showing white and even teeth. He gave a little gesture of recognition, which, after a moment's hesitation, made Graham ask him politely if he had found everything all right so far; it was rather an awkward line for losing luggage on.

'Yes, yes, thanks, all right so far. It is no joke, however, travelling about

A Girl's Past. 31

with such a pile, and four unprotected females into the bargain. But I'm used to it—we are birds of passage, old hands at travelling. I am going down as *locum tenens* for an invalided parson, and, as the engagement will last some time, I have to bring a heap of "portable property."'

'Ah! In the neighbourhood of Erdley?'

'In Erdley itself, sir. We are bound for Erdley Rectory.'

'For the Rectory? Is Merryweather ill, then?'

'Yes, sir, he is. Ordered abroad at once for the chest—to travel a year or two. I knew him formerly, so he was glad to engage me. You know Merryweather, then?'

'Yes, very well; it is odd I had not heard he was ill. I think, sir, you had better get into the train now, it soon starts. Good-afternoon.'

They separated, each wondering a little about the other. So this smooth-spoken, seedy-looking parson, with the (slightly) red nose and the taste for 'modest quenchers,' as Dick Swiveller puts it, was bound for Erdley Rectory, the pompous, old-fashioned, drily — irreproachable Merryweather was his complete antithesis.

Mr Lane meanwhile bundled his ladies and their parcels pell-mell into a new train. Once settled there, he began—he and his fair-haired daughter were the talkers of the party,—

'I saw that nice-looking, gentlemanly, young fellow again, and he spoke very civilly. I wonder who he can be. Erdley is an uncommonly small place; he must be going to stay with one of the county families, I suppose. He has nothing of the swell about him, yet there is an air —a something— I hope we may meet at Erdley. Madge, my dear, I really should be obliged to you not to kick my shins.'

The little lame girl blushed, and apologised. She was beginning to look very tired, and her eldest sister quietly made a sort of cushion of herself, against which the aching little back could rest, while she picked up her feet, curled them on the seat, and put a shawl over them.

'Is that better, Madge?' she said, in a low-toned, sad, contralto voice, just the voice that ought to belong to her face.

The little girl glanced at her with a grateful smile.

'Ever so much better, Gwen.'

Then, as the father and other sister chatted on discursively from one topic to another, with an occasional remark from the mother, Gwen's dark eyes fell, and she was as quiet and passive as if asleep.

At Erdley station Mr Lane watched, with as much attention as he could spare from collecting his heterogeneous mass of bundles, boxes and baskets, and stowing them into a fusty and ancient omnibus, which was waiting for his party, to see the 'gentlemanly young fellow' depart. A high dog-cart was waiting, driven by a young groom, into which Graham climbed, after tipping the porters liberally, as appeared from their wreathèd smiles, but Mr Lane failed to discover his final destination.

A Girl's Past.

The village of Erdley was about a mile from the station, the church and parsonage still a little farther on. The crazy old vehicle jolted the weary bodies of the dusty, rather forlorn-looking little party over the hard, stony road.

Mrs Lane was resignedly tired and patient as usual, her husband snappish and captious, Madge half worn out, Ettie cross, Gwen — well, Gwen was simply silent, but she looked weary enough. The village was rather a large one. It boasted a butcher's shop, of which the stock-in-trade appeared to be a dangling, objectionable-looking bullock's heart, and a lean, wizen shoulder of mutton. The blue-frocked butcher commented on the omnibus and its occupants, as it passed, to his neighbour, who kept a combined grocery, boot and shoe and china shop, which he called an Emporium. The widow over the way, who baked for the parish, looked out also and hoped there would be a good consumption of bread now at the Vicarage, Mr Merryweather and his two servants had eaten scandalously little.

The post-office, which was also a stationer's, was the only other shop in the long straggling street. The doctor's and lawyer's houses stood cheek by jowl with their shining brass plates; an 'Establishment for Young Ladies' towered above the small tenements on each side. The street was wide, grass-grown, unexciting. Then came a few more scattered houses and cottages, then, in a cluster, the stumpy brown tower of the church, a rather snug-looking vicarage, whose garden opened on to the churchyard, which, however, was a sunshiny and pleasant one, and a substantial farm-house, whose out-buildings and yards were flanked and shaded by a group of elms. The rooks swung and cawed there pleasantly in spring-time.

'Here we are, thank goodness! Not a bad-looking house either,' cried the clergyman, as he surveyed his temporary resting-place.

Mrs Lane looked out with an inward sigh. Oh, if only this homelike place could have been a real home! If only her dreary wanderings from place to place might be over and she could sit permanently by a familiar hearth. But her life had grown to be a meek acceptance of the inevitable. 'What good does talking do?' was the formula of her existence.

'Get out, girls, hurry up!' the father cried impatiently, as they collected their belongings. 'Let us see if there is anything to be had to eat. We have had a day of it with these wearisome cross-country journeys.'

A rustic-looking woman-servant, the 'General' whom Mrs Lane had engaged to help on domestic concerns, opened the door, with sleeves tucked up above her bare, red arms. She dipped an awkward curtsey, and came forward to help with the luggage. Tea and cold meat was ready in the long, low, oak-panelled dining-room. The furniture was solid and respectably old-fashioned. The place looked kindly.

'It's all very nice, I'm sure,' Mrs Lane said, in her slow, languid voice, naturally pitched, like Gwen's, in a minor key. 'Such a sweet country smell.'

'Yes, it's very well, very well,' her husband said, dancing and fidgeting about in his usual restless, rapid fashion. 'Don't stop to unpack or any nonsense now, Esther. Let's have tea directly; we all want it. Then we'll go over the house and see what room there is in it for pupils.'

At that Mrs Lane's mouth drooped again and she sighed. Her connections with the word were all dismal. Too well she knew what that oft-repeated phrase, 'Mr Lane's pupils,' meant. It had almost power enough to take away the flavour of her tea, which was the one luxury of her toiling life. The meal despatched, the girls went to settle their bedrooms. Ettie—so the second one was invariably called—always slept alone; Gwen choosing to take the care of the delicate little sister, who was her pet and nursling.

She had to be helped to bed, laying her aching, tired little dark head down on the pillow, which smelt of rosemary and lavender, with a sigh of content.

'How *clean* it all is,' she said admiringly. 'Leave the blind up, Gwen; there's a nice bit of sky, and the tops of some trees. They rest me. It's a dear old room, isn't it, Gwen? only so many cupboards. Please look in *all* of them before you go down, and lock them this side. There might be—something in them.'

'But there isn't, see,' Gwen said,

throwing open first one door in the wall then another. 'There's one more, but that's locked up. They have left things in it, I suppose.'

'Oh, dear!' Madge cried, raising her head from her pillow. 'I *wish* there wasn't a locked cupboard in the room one doesn't know anything about! Perhaps—perhaps there's a skeleton inside it, Gwen.'

'My dear, there's always one in *our* cupboard,' Gwen returned, half laughing, but not mirthfully.

She was sorry the next moment for having said it. Her nervous little sister took her too literally

'Oh, Gwen! Not really?'

'No, no, dear; I was only talking nonsense. There is nothing here I am sure but old clothes.'

'How can you know? How can you be sure?'

'Yes, yes, I know. But I am not going down anyhow. I will sit by the window here till you're asleep, I've something to mend. You mustn't be a goose, Madge. No one is ever afraid of anything in the country.'

Madge subsided, soothed by the promise of companionship.

Before very long she had forgotten the weariness of her poor little body, which, too often, was to her but a vehicle for pain, and was dreaming of an impossible land where pain was not, nor the terrors of the everyday life.

Gwen sat and stared out of the window on the darkening landscape.

Her work had been a pretence. There was no light to sew by, and she was too listless and tired to light a candle.

The autumn day had died. Presently a broad red moon almost startled her by a sudden glimpse of brightness amongst the elm trees. It was a solemn, peaceful look-out. The light reflected itself in Gwen's great deep dark eyes as in the pool beyond the farmyard. Her pale, pretty sad face looked spiritualised and beautiful in the moonshine. It was a pity to see anyone so young, yet with nothing of the hope or joy of youth about her. In repose Gwen looked more pathetic even than in ordinary moments, and at no time could anyone fail to be struck by the wistfulness of her expression and the cast of her features. Perhaps it was but a trick, a freak of Nature's; perhaps that look meant nothing more than that she had inherited a colourless complexion, a shape of face, a certain mould of mouth, and unsmiling deep eyes, which had really no connection with mournful ideas or events. Perhaps. I do not open Gwen's mind to you. She followed the rise of the great red moon as it changed its hue to a paler gold, and an hour drifted by before she could make up her mind to leave her quiet watch and join her mother and sister in the unpacking that was necessary for the night. An impatient call from her sister woke her from her dream. With a sigh she went out into the candle-light and the wearisome bustle of arrangement.

CHAPTER III.

GRAHAM felt a certain natural elation of heart as the dog-cart drew up at the stone portico of his own house. He glanced round with a new, agreeable sense of possession. It was not a 'lordly pleasure house,' nor a vast estate, simply an old-fashioned, solid, comfortable-looking, red-brick country mansion, of no particular style of architecture, beautified by climbing roses in front, and virginia creepers on the sides, with a goodly array of small-paned, white eye-browed windows, and with a hospitable open door, which admitted into a pleasant, square, carpeted hall, where a fire of logs was burning, which looked hospitable though it was warm weather. The gardens were not very extensive, but prettily planted with fine large shrubs and trees, and with a smooth expanse of mossy lawn, divided with a gap and sunken wall from the paddock or small park beyond. Rogers, his cousin's man-servant, a rather lugubrious-looking, but eminently respectable elderly man, with grey whiskers neatly trimmed to his thin long face, came forward, with an air of grave decorous welcome, as his new master sprang lightly to the ground and offered him his hand with that cordial simplicity which was one of the secrets of his attraction.

'Here I am! How are you, Rogers? All ready for me?'

'Quite ready sir; all well, thank you, sir. Allow me. Mr Willoughby, sir, is within. Oh, here he is. He thought you might feel a little lonely the first evening, so came in to dinner.'

'Ha, that's right! How are you Mr Willoughby? Very kind of you to take compassion on me!'

Mr Willoughby, the owner of a small property adjoining the Manor House, had been Mr Graham's chief, if not only friend in Erdley, and had been left his executor. In spite of a difference of nearly thirty years in their ages, the present owner of the Manor House and he were also friends.

Mr Willoughby was a remarkably tall thin man of stork-like proportions, so shy, diffident and nervous, that he had adopted various strange, restless tricks and movements, which rendered him uncouth, though never unrefined. Odd, loose, shabby in dress, and by no means handsome, yet he had an air of distinction, and could never have been mistaken for anything but a perfect gentleman. A love of books and dislike of ordinary society had been points of sympathy between him and the late Mr Graham; but Mr Willoughby had other traits, which were more congenial to the younger Graham. He was a thorough country lover, fond of sport, of shooting, fishing and riding, an authority on all rustic lore. Graham liked his wife also; for, though Mr Willoughby had been too shy and too vacillating to make up his mind to marry till he had most of the habits and the years of an old bachelor, he had at last got a wife, a maiden lady no longer young, whom he had liked for years and might have married long before if he had not been too nervous to ask her, and she too dignified to encourage him. However, when they did manage a serious, sedate, middle-aged marriage, they were happy in a quiet unsentimental way. Mrs Willoughby, who was fond of society of the unexciting kind, gently coerced her husband into hospitality, and was sympathetic with young people, even though they often surprised and not a little shocked her with their emancipated ways.

Mr Willoughby greeted his friend with as much cordiality as his queer, jerky, nervous manner would permit to appear, and when the first awkwardness, which he always experienced with acquaintances, was spent, he became communicative.

He was ready to join Graham in a day's pheasant shooting on the morrow, which his wife insisted was to end in the young man dining with them. The birds were plentiful, and prospects of sport good. The news of the estate and business affairs occupied the early part of the dinner, which was a simple one enough, but well cooked, as Mrs Rogers was accustomed to serve her old master who had some fastidious tastes. Then Graham had questions to ask about his neighbours. He had not been down now for two and a half years, and there were a few changes, though but few.

'Dick Hall drank himself to death. It was a great grief to the old people.

I fear the younger brother is rather inclined the same way. That pretty, consumptive Miss Ray died a year ago. Young Willard married a good-looking, fast girl, whom my wife abhors —a Miss Cooke, from near Stroud. It was a pity, for he's a nice fellow. They have a noisy, racketty house. The Miss Barnetts are unmarried still. Look out for yourself with them, Graham. They will all be ready to pounce; and if you are at all attentive, mamma will ask your intentions. I believe that's about the extent of Erdley news.'

'Stay; there's a change at the Vicarage, isn't there?'

'To be sure. Stupid of me to forget that important item. Merryweather quite broke down, poor fellow; had a long illness in the spring, and is ordered abroad to take some years' rest. He has got a *locum tenens* for two years, I believe. I heard he was to come to-day.'

'He did; in the same train with me, also a wife and three daughters, name of Lane.'

'Ay, that was it. He was at college with Merryweather, or school, or something. A High Churchman rather, and a clever man, I've heard, but I know nothing more of him.'

'I suppose I ought to call on *him*, not he on me, eh?'

'I don't know. I daresay it might be kind. We shall see what he's like on Sunday; and the wife and I must call. It will be somewhat of a relief if the fellow can preach, for old Merryweather can't. He ground out one or two tunes, like a barrel-organ; we had pretty well exhausted him. But he is a good, well-meaning man.'

'Oh, very; only a bore. I'm sorry he's in bad health.'

A pause devoted to port wine and filberts, then from Mr Willoughby,—

'Come to make a long stay, Graham?'

'I don't know. I have left all my plans indefinite. It is rather jolly to feel no one has any right to control one's actions. I resigned the office a month ago.'

'And feel like Prince Fortunatus?'

'I feel it's a pleasant position, but I don't suppose I shall find it all play.'

'Not if you go in for conscientious squire work — try new theories and study grievances. There'll always be folks to grumble, and want you to do no end of things. You'll either have to ignore or to tackle the "duties of your position," which people talk so much of. Poor old Graham shut himself up, and tried to shut his ears. He always said he was like Hamlet, not born to set things right. You're young, and energetic, and, I fancy, a bit fond of theories. I daresay you will feel that *you* are. Meanwhile, get your fun out of it while you can. You've got a good managing man in Grant, only he's a little hard and narrow. Don't let him tyrannise over you.'

Graham felt his will strong and his mind capable enough to enter on his responsibilities with courage. Things looked bright through the rosy medium of the bottle of fine old port which Rogers had unearthed for the occasion. Life was full of interest, from pheasant shooting to pretty girls. He had zest for all forms of distraction. These two daughters of the new clergyman were both of them very pretty, even in the unbecoming dust and shabbiness of their travelling costumes. They would be prettier still in a more favourable moment. He quite looked forward to the call he contemplated paying on the first decent opportunity ; then he could make up his mind on the point which perplexed him—which style was most attractive ; the fair-haired, blue-eyed, lively type, or the dark, pale and sad one. He wondered *why* that girl had such a melancholy expression. She was too young, surely, to have come by it naturally. Years of sorrow alone could justify the lonely, dreamy depths of her eyes—a trick, probably—an accident of feature. Some quite ordinary people have a way of looking pathetic. He should not be at all surprised to find Miss Lane a dull, common-place sort of girl after all; the other one must certainly be amusing. As a rule, he was drawn to lively people.

The next day he and Mr Willoughby 'pouthered up and down' after the pheasants, 'and had a rattlin' day' in the plantations and over the fields and sides of Loxeter Hill. The pop pop of the guns were frequent, and the bag heavy. A great many brace found their way to different houses, with 'Mr Graham Brooke-Graham's' new card attached.

He was delighted to find his eye as true and his aim as sure as ever. Clean, wholesome living had left his body strong, muscular and in excellent case. Mrs Willoughby, a rather faded, yet nice-looking, lady-like woman, the dignity of whose manners was tempered by solicitous kindness, received him cordially in the drawing-room she had managed to make so very like herself, quiet-toned, comfortable, and in good taste, with nothing obtrusive or fine about it. She liked Graham with all her heart, as middle-aged and old ladies always did. He took trouble to be polite to them, and had a frank open-heartedness in speech and manner, with yet a kind of reserve which prevented his being seen through too easily, which was agreeable to those who are apt to expect little from young men. She had been 'doing her district' in the village as she told them, and had met the new people from the Vicarage in the post-office. 'A fussy little man, very quick and talkative, moves his hand a great deal, and is rather oratorical, a worn-out, pale-looking wife, and a very pretty fair daughter.'

'Oh, you saw only the *fair* daughter!' cried Graham, displaying a sudden interest. 'There is another—a perfect contrast—but both are very pretty. Rather nice sort of people don't you think, Mrs Willoughby? Only very poor, I should suppose?'

'Yes, very poor, I fancy. I don't know that I took *much* to the clergyman. One ought not to judge, but *locum tenens*, you know, are apt to be—'

She broke off with an apologetic little laugh as she saw her husband was writhing and squeezing up his eyes, signs she had learnt to understand as well as words.

'Leigh thinks me uncharitable and censorious,' she said to Graham, smiling; 'don't you Leigh? He has a theory that all women are.'

'No, no, don't pay yourself bad compliments and father them on me. Only don't let us start with the idea, first that *locum tenens* are, as a rule, objectionable, secondly, Mr Lane is a *locum tenens, ergo* Mr Lane is objectionable. His poverty, perhaps not his will, offends. The Church has not prizes to offer everybody; there are unlucky dogs in every profession. Merryweather is a cautious man, he would not have asked this one to come, I expect, if he had not known he was all right. And, at any rate,' he added quaintly, with an odd twitch of his eyes in the young man's direction, 'Lane has two pretty daughters, Graham says. There's safety in numbers; stick to the two, my boy.'

'Well, we may count it to him as a virtue, mayn't we? till we know of some others,' Graham rejoined, smiling. 'It's better to have pretty daughters than ugly ones. I feel rather inclined to be sorry for our new temporary parson, do you know, there was such an air of seediness about the whole turn-out of the family. It can't be a cheerful life.'

'*He* looks cheerful enough,' Mrs Willoughby put in. 'Rather over lively. The wife has a sad face.'

'Well, I daresay it is worst for the wife if they're poor. It generally is worse for the women in this world.'

'Where did yon learn your philosophy, my boy?' Mr Willoughby asked laughing his odd, short, spasmodic little laugh. 'You've no vast experience of women.'

'From my mother, I suppose,' Graham answered, rather gravely. 'We were very poor once, she had a hard struggle of it when my father died. At any rate I always feel glad that the Fates did not make me a woman.'

'Well,' Mrs Willoughby said in her quiet, decisive voice, 'there are women, on the other hand, who rejoice not to be men. I am one of them.'

'Yes, I daresay the best women

would agree with you, the nicest certainly of them would.'

'*Merci du compliment!*' she said, smiling at him. 'I don't find fault with the strong-minded ladies, the emancipated ones, but I have no inclination for the *rôle*. I hope, to go back to the new clergyman, that Mrs Lane and her daughters will prove to be pleasant and useful. We always wished poor Mr Merryweather had a wife. There is plenty to do in Erdley.'

'Mrs Lane did not look much like a *doer*, I thought. But what can there be to do in Erdley, Mrs Willoughby?'

'There are a great many very poor people, and of rather a low type—' Mrs Willoughby began.

Her husband interrupted her a little tartly.

A Girl's Past.

'To pauperise and lower still further—to encourage in lies and begging! My wife, Graham, is the most absurdly generous, the most mischievous of givers. She would ruin the whole parish if I gave her her head.'

'Well, dear,' his wife put in with a tone of serene protest, 'you are always raving about the bad housing and bad pay, I am sure. And if one can make poor people a little happier, it can't be very wrong to do it.'

'Right or wrong you'll continue to go your own way,' he retorted, with a twist and a writhe.

'I am afraid I shall. I am too old to be reformed;' and, smiling pleasantly on them both, the mild-mannered, kindly, but persistent woman left them to their wine.

CHAPTER IV.

THE next day was Sunday. Graham had knocked about the world and seen the noisy side of it too much to be unable to relish the large calm, the profound leisure, the brooding peace of a sunshiny country Sunday. One fancies that if one were dropped on a rural spot of earth from another planet, this day would be instantly recognisable. The very sky seemed washed, like the doorsteps and the children's faces; the quiet air was only broken in upon by the sound of bells. The rooks cawed a lazy chorus from the churchyard elms; the hens seemed to put on a Sabbatical cluck for the day; the cock crowed like a hoarse, respectable parish clerk. Graham's two pet dogs, Trim and Dainty, looked up at him with wistful protest when he appeared in his black Sunday coat with a flower in it. Why would people go flocking once a week to a big grey house where dogs are not admitted? Graham had not been a great church-goer, but, for various reasons, he intended to-day to take his seat in the Squire's pew. He stood on the doorstep, listening to the bells, after breakfast, snuffing up the sweet, still autumn morning, and drawing on a respectable pair of gloves, which Trim would much have liked to tear to pieces. Dressed in these irreproachable London clothes, with his sunburnt, manly, sweet-tempered face and golden brown moustache, broad-shouldered, well set on a pair of straight, firm legs, Mr Graham Brooke-Graham appeared a very personable young man indeed, though he had no legitimate claims to beauty. He patted the dogs, and condoled with them as he gave his orders to them to stay behind, and repressed the eager little rushes they could not help making to follow.

'After lunch, old chaps, you shall have a run. We're on Sunday behaviour remember;' and he strode off, swinging his stick, no dandy cane but a good thick, knobby affair which had accompanied his wanderings for years.

As he fell in with scattered groups along the road, all going towards the stumpy-towered church, he met with

A Girl's Past. 67

various greetings, curtseys and bows to the 'young squire,' 'how d'ye do's,' and polite small remarks from such of the higher class as he knew, sweet smiles and volleys of glances in the porch where the four Miss Barnetts were shaking out their plumage — very smart plumage, too, though it was the end of the summer, for they had made a special effort for the occasion of Mr Brooke - Graham's first appearance in that character. Graham was polite but stoical; the Miss Barnetts did not, as he expressed it, 'fetch him' at all.

He entered the cool - smelling, old-fashioned village sanctuary and walked to his place under a fire of glances, blushing a little, perhaps, but with steadfast unwavering eyes. It was a primitive little place, untouched by the professional restorer, with black oak pews, irregular paving, and a low, humble altar, for which Mrs Willoughby had lately worked a cloth; with a narrow lancet painted window above, and vases filled with late flowers. Mr Merryweather was one of the old school, and though he rather liked ritual he had not had energy enough to change time-honoured customs, so there was a mixed choir of village girls, boys and men, and the old clerk, though his office was nearly a sinecure, still led the Amens and responses. The Parsonage pew was occupied. Graham's was just opposite, and he naturally glanced at the new family. Mrs Lane, in thin black silk that crackled like paper, and a bonnet that had seen good service, sat at the end, the lame little girl beside her, then came Ettie in a blue bonnet which set off the golden hair which fluffed prettily about her vivacious fair face. She managed to look nice, though, as Miss Barnett whispered to her sister, 'she had got nothing on worth two-pence halfpenny.'

What did Graham's manly mind know of cost or fabric? He thought the cheap cream-coloured costume looked very well, and was confirmed in his impression of her prettiness.

But where was the 'dark one'? He glanced about and discovered that she sat at the small organ, half hidden by a scanty curtain. She played the voluntary well, but he fancied she was very nervous over it. Then Mr Lane's resonant, though worn, musical voice began in a strong, sure intoning, 'When the wicked man,' and all the congregation were on their feet. They were not used to intoning. Some of the old-world folks, who dreaded popery, did not like it, nor any of the innovations which it was evident Mr Lane intended to make law, but Graham was pleased with the service. It was much more musical and harmonious than he remembered of yore. Mr Lane not only intoned well, he sang also, loud, in a sure, rather fine if worn baritone. Ettie, too, raised a high, clear, true soprano, which dominated the uncertain voices which at once followed and obeyed her lead.

It was evident the new family were musical. Graham could detect, besides the fresh treble, a rich, full contralto making itself heard as a thrush does in a chorus of shriller birds. It came from the young organist. He was pleased with the fitness of things that gave the fair, gay-looking sister her clear, high, canary notes, and the sad-faced one that pathetic, rich contralto. Ettie genuflected, curtseyed, and performed various rites, yet her demeanour was not reverential. She turned her slender throat from right to left, observing everything and everybody. More than once Graham met shrewd glances from the blue eyes opposite. He was amused with the lively girl, with her outward gestures of devotion and her evident wide-awakeness to secular fact. If she had been less pretty he might have been a little more severe on the light behaviour of a girl who ought to have 'set an example' as clergyman's daughter. Theresa, Charlotte, Ada, and Genevieve Barnett were, however, *very* severe, and that made the balance even. The sermon was short, which in itself was a recommendation after the long service, but it was also distinctly a good sermon. Mr Lane had a fine pulpit voice, and made it sympathetic; the matter was well turned, sensible, and rather impressive. Graham felt inclined to rejoice over poor Mr Merryweather's misfortunes. He made up his mind to call at the Parsonage the very next day, whatever etiquette might say was the proper thing, of which he was not sure. He stopped behind the rest of the congregation to introduce himself to the Lanes. They had already found out all about their fellow-traveller, and the clergyman responded warmly to his salutation. He, in his turn, begged to introduce Mrs Lane, his daughters, Gweneth, Esther and Margaret, for they appeared at full length on state occasions. They walked together a short distance, and Mr Lane was very chatty and communicative. He was glad Mr Brooke-Graham had liked the service. There was a great deal he should wish to reform, but must go softly to work, as he was only a stop-gap. Merryweather, no doubt, was an excellent man, a little fossilised. For his part he liked a rather ornate service, plenty of music and good music. Yes, they *were* a musical lot. He supposed there was no vanity in saying that. It was born in them all. His wife once sang magnificently ('You did, my dear,' to a feeble protest). She had lost her voice, but still played the piano better than most people. Gwen played the organ and sang; Ettie the violin, and had a good pipe of her own; Madge was learning the 'cello. The boys (he had two boys at school), were musical too. He himself had some taste. Did Mr Brooke-Graham relish music? Ah, if so, he must help at their little family concerts. They intended to get up village musical entertainments, popular but refined. The bucolic taste needed educating.

He talked so fast there was not much

A Girl's Past. 75

chance of getting in more than a word or two, but Graham was not loquacious. He listened, and considered Mr Lane a bit bumptious and underbred, perhaps, but well-meaning—a good-natured, rather clever little man. The ladies of the party were silent enough, with the exception of Esther, who tried now and then to get her oar in. She was much the most like the father. She evidently wanted to start a friendship with Mr Brooke - Graham, and he was quite cordial and ready. Gwen, with Madge clinging to her arm as she limped along with her little crutch, walked in silence. He hardly heard her voice at all. She glanced about her, and the beauty of the day and scene seemed to find a reflection in her looks, which softened and brightened a little out of their usual sombre quietude. Now and then she said a word under her breath to her little sister, making her notice a peep of view, a scudding rabbit, or yellowing tree, but that was all. She seemed either very shy, very reserved, or very — no, she was *not* stupid. She had a sympathetic nature, or her eyes would not have dwelt so lovingly on the beautiful things of the country. Graham spoke of calling as they reached the parting of their ways, and Mr Lane warmly and fussily invited him to come and have a—a cup of tea, he added, as he met his wife's warning look, with them any day at five o'clock or so.

'To-morrow?' asked Graham.

'Certainly! To-morrow, by all means. They were pretty straight, as straight

A Girl's Past. 77

as poor wanderers can be,' he added, sighing.

'I often pray for a quiet, permanent haven, Mr Brooke-Graham, but I have never had any luck. From pillar to post, that has been my fate.'

He sighed again, but still he looked cheerful enough.

Graham fancied the sigh was echoed in poor Mrs Lane's heart if not on her patient lips. Mr Lane waved his hand at parting from his new friend as if they had known each other for years.

'Shall we have to be forever "Brooke-Grahaming" him?' asked Ettie. 'It's a ridiculous double-barrelled name.'

'I wonder if he'd mind plain Graham,' mused Mrs Lane. 'It *is* a mouthful.'

'You had better give him the benefit of his hyphen, as it means a good deal to him,' Mr Lane said. 'He was only a poor War Office clerk before, I hear. This is a nice little property.'

'What is a "hyphen," Gwen?' whispered Madge. 'I learnt in "Mary's Grammar," I think, but I forget.'

'A little line that joins two words,' Gwen answered, briefly.

Madge's education was elementary and precarious. She had never been to school or had a governess. Gwen taught her what little she could 'when there was time.'

'Well, what has that got to do with that gentleman?'

'His name used to be Brooke, now it is Brooke-Graham with a hyphen.'

'Why?'

Madge loved to know the whys and wherefores of things.

'Because a Mr Graham left him money, he took the name.'

'Is he rich, then?'

'I suppose he is, rather.'

'Richer than father?'

'You silly child! You know we are not rich *at all*. We are very poor.'

'How many pounds a year make people rich?'

'Madge, don't bother with questions. I can't tell you.'

Gwen spoke rather irritably. She had not the best of tempers. No one of the Lanes had, except the long-suffering mother, but then she was never spiteful or 'nasty,' and Madge never loved her less for occasional moments of irritation which did not last. Gwen was at once her heroine and her darling.

She admired, adored and served her with intense, unspoken devotion.

Mr Lane had by this time dropped the subject of Brooke-Graham, and was speaking in his rapid, skimming, impatient sort of way of two pupils he expected by the end of the month.

'I wish we need not have them,' his wife sighed, half afraid when she had spoken.

He turned angrily upon her.

'Don't you suppose *I* wish so too? Isn't it a nuisance, a hateful infliction on *me?* I wish you would tell me *how* to avoid it. I wish to heaven I could earn £200 a year any other way. Isn't it worse for me than you?'

Mrs Lane did not answer. She could not. She could not truthfully say that she thought so. Her husband could

A Girl's Past. 81

shake them off, could go out and forget them. He had such a delightfully easy way of forgetting evils. *She* never could. Their presence was a misery and an incubus to her all day long.

But why did the innocent word 'pupil' suggest such ideas to her mind? Why not rather a mild image of a theological student, a sort of acolyte, soft of speech, meek of bearing? Alas! Mr Lane's pupils were not of this kind. He advertised for 'troublesome youths.' Parents wearied and hopeless of reform sent him their black sheep. Truly, his hundred per annum was hardly earned.

They had had every variety of *mauvais sujet*, from dunce to dipsomaniac, and everyone had left a new wrinkle of sadness on Mrs Lane's careworn countenance. She suffered and submitted. Her husband had a faculty of taking things easy, though he let off a good deal of steam in complaints and self-pity.

There was Irish blood as well as fiery Welsh in Mr Lane, and the former was accountable for the incorrigible hopefulness which had carried him over many a bad passage. He was often in the depths of despair, but a good dinner, an extra glass of whisky-and-water, a quarterly payment, would suffice to raise his spirits, and the mere satisfaction of talking and grumbling about his misfortune to a willing listener was always a consolation. And he had an unshakeably good opinion of himself, that had survived many a shock which would have utterly prostrated a less robust conceit. In these things lay the secret of Mr Lane's frequent joviality, which really had little excuse, as could well be supposed.

He had some grounds, however, for conceit. He really was a clever man; the marvel was, he had never found a better market for his talents. A fine voice and delivery, a quickness of invention, and a very tolerable amount of learning ought to have landed him in the secure haven of a comfortable living, but somehow no one ever could quite trust him for long together. He was unstable as water, and often managed to gain credit for positive vices which he did not possess. A violent, if easily appeased temper, and a habit of inaccuracy of speech, generally made themselves seen, and did him more harm than the 'ill luck,' which he freely denounced as the sole origin of all his disasters. His long-suffering, gentle and, on the whole, affectionate wife, though she no longer cherished illusions about him, still managed to preserve enough kindness for him to excuse the faults she never attempted not to see.

Of all his children he cared most for Ettie, of whom he was proud, who resembled him, and had the audacity to beard him in his most irritable moods. He admired, was proud of her, and intended her to marry well. He was not long in informing his wife, in the privacy of the matrimonial chamber, that Brooke-Graham certainly admired Ettie. He looked at her a long while, and with approval. It would be a nice match for the girl.

'But if it were Gwen,' his wife faltered timidly.

Mr Lane bristled into wrath in a moment, and was positive, as he always was, in defence of his most unsupported theories.

'Gwen? Nonsense! he hardly looked at Gwen. Ettie is the girl to attract a young fellow like that. You have always something uncomfortable to suggest, Esther.'

CHAPTER V.

THE very next day Graham paid his promised call at the Parsonage. The prim, old-fashioned order of Mr Merryweather's regime was already displaced. Signs of a family, and a not very orderly one, were broadcast over the whole house. Doors stood open, hats and jackets were thrown on to the umbrella-stand that had been only used to the vicar's soft black hat and sedate overcoat; the drawing-room was full of unaccustomed lumber, music on the chairs and on the square old piano, a violoncello case leant against the wall, some feminine work and a dilapidated novel were on the table. Mrs Lane sat near the window sewing; Madge was in the garden outside on a bench with her doll; the other girls appeared from somewhere. The visitor was not sorry to find the father of the family absent. Where he was there was a little chance of hearing any other voice. It proved to be Ettie's chiefly that was heard in default of his; she decidedly took the lead. Though only eighteen years old, Miss Ettie was a very self-confident young person, and seldom at a loss. She laughed a great deal, showing a glimpse of regular white young teeth and a pretty dimple that came and went. She was friendly, nay intimate, in a minute—no ice to break here. The other two were quite different. Mrs Lane was nervous, diffident, never at her ease with outsiders, apt to be apologetic, and to seem unsure of herself and her position.' She had no conversation, and an awkward manner. Gwen, too, though not awkward, was singularly silent and reserved. She let Ettie rattle on, and made no effort to take an elder sister's share in entertaining a pleasant young man. Graham was piqued. He wanted to hear her low, sad-toned, melodious voice oftener. He wanted to find out if she were proud, stupid, shy, or unhappy, to fathom the meaning that seemed to lie deep in the large, dark, liquid eyes which he seldom met in a straight open glance.

Were ever sisters more unlike? The old hackneyed contrasts of night and morning, sunshine and shadow, rose to the mind involuntarily. What had made one so grave, the other so gay? Probably temperament, forces as unaccountable as tinted their eyes and gave the different calibre to their voices.

A look and whisper from her mother sent Gwen presently out of the room, and after enough time for boiling some water had elapsed, the one servant appeared with a tray, Gwen following, a little flushed, which a glance at the toast which accompanied the tea accounted for.

Graham was struck suddenly by the positive beauty which this delicate rose colour gave the pale, still face. That and a sudden smile, which something he said brought out, were all that was required to make her lovely. It was a pity to see both colour and smile fade so quickly.

Mr Lane made his appearance soon after the tea, and began to eat toast and to talk with equal rapidity. He was very suave and agreeable to his guest, and really knew how to converse well on a good many discursive subjects in a sketchy but telling way. He had for the last five years been in London, but before that he had travelled a good deal, taking chaplaincies in various continental towns. Graham and he found interest in comparing notes on places they both knew. Ettie kept a robust hold on the conversation, however, not allowing it to become a duologue, but the other two members of the family who were present, as usual retired into the background. They seemed interested in each other, and had a low remark now and then to interchange on some small, domestic matter. After tea Graham reminded his host that he had been promised music.

Mr Lane was perfectly willing to show off the accomplishments of his family.

'What will you have? A duet? Gwen's and Ettie's voices go admirably together. It is really a kind provision of nature that gave Ettie a high soprano and Gwen a contralto. Here are the old favourites—Mendelssohn. Choose one for them!'

Graham chose the old hackneyed duet, which he loved for the words as well as the music, 'Wert thou in the cauld blast.'

He never afterwards disassociated it with Gwen. She had the saddest, richest of contralto voices, which lent a new pathos to what was already pathetic. After that Ettie sang. They had a stock of old standard music, the regular repertoire of well-trained amateurs, but nothing very new. Ettie gave them 'Cherry ripe,' 'Where the bee sucks,' and so on. Her high, bird-like trill was very pretty, but he was impatient for the deeper, sadder voice, and was ready, when the younger sister had done, with a book of Kingsley's ballads for the elder. He made Gwen sing 'The Sands o' Dee,' the 'Three Fishers,' 'Oh that we two were maying.' Like many happy young people he loved to be thrilled into sympathetic melancholy. The dark-eyed, ivory-pale girl puzzled him. *What* made her look so mournful? *Why* was she so utterly reserved, so apart from the rest? He hardly heard her father speak to her, all his talk was directed to the favourite, gay, pretty, smiling Ettie. Graham found the younger sister perfectly approachable, friendly, coquettish, lively. He only got monosyllables from Gwen. She did not seem at all vain of her musical powers; she sang because she was asked, perhaps because singing was easier than talking, besides, it was the thing to be done, what visitors expected. Her father did not discuss her. He answered Graham's question about the organ by saying Gwen had undertaken it for the present as they seemed in difficulties. He hoped amongst them they should make a decent choir in time, but the country voices were not musical. Gwen would start a class of boys.

'How shall you like that?' Graham asked her.

'Oh, very well,' she answered, in her low-pitched indifferent voice. 'They will be troublesome, I daresay, but I have done it before.'

'It must be trying work—it is rough material.'

'Yes. But I sha'n't mind.'

'I wonder what would bring her out of her shell,' Graham thought as he walked home, with the rich voice echoing in his mind. 'What would make that girl break out into a rage—or a fit of laughter—or—or anything but that dull dreary calm? She must be very young, perhaps twenty, but she hasn't a scrap of the gaiety of youth about her. Is she miserable at home? Poor they are, no doubt. The mother looks care-ridden enough, but is there worse than poverty? Is the father a secret tyrant, does he beat or swear at them? No, there's no appearance of anything actually bad in him—a bit of a windbag, perhaps a humbug, but no look of cruelty or wickedness. Still, I don't fancy he and she are on the best of terms. I wish I could find out what gives her that unhappy look!'

Graham hated to see suffering, especially in women, children or animals. He was no sentimentalist. He had seen men die in a skirmish, he had faced many a danger sternly enough, but the misery of an ill-used child, the cry of a wounded dog, the sorrow in a woman's eyes 'made a fool of him,' as he said. He tried to think that Gwen was only made to look so by a cast of feature, by natural complexion, yet still his thoughts recurred to her, and he still vexed his mind with conjectures as to causes where perhaps none were to be found. It was certainly odd that two sisters should be so utterly unlike, but heredity will account for any strange diversity. The one had the temperament of one branch of ancestors, the other of a different race. He himself and Kitty generally disagreed about things. But in spite of all reasoning he felt he should be glad if he could make Gweneth Lane look happy.

The splendid autumn weather showed no signs yet of giving way to the

A Girl's Past.

dominion of winter; though October it was positively hot. One day, soon after this, Graham felt almost fagged out, after a long ramble with his gun and dogs, and was glad to strike into the shade of the small plantation that skirted the lower part of his garden, and which was generally called the Wilderness. This part of the Erdley Manor House property was only vaguely protected from trespassers by a casual board announcing that such 'would be prosecuted,' and, as a fact, the Erdley people made pretty free with the Wilderness, which could be easily entered from the high road. In spring the largest and finest primroses, oxlips, and blue hyacinths grew here. In summer their kingdom was taken by a host of lordly foxgloves, below these the pink stars of campion and the white of stitchwort made a gay tapestry. Now but few flowers remained; not much beside a little honeysuckle, some traveller's joy, and some other isolated blossoms, but the berries were beginning to show colour and to tempt the children's clutch. Graham was hot and tired. He threw himself on a bed of pine needles, sniffed in the warm, aromatic air, and lay staring at the blue sky that peeped through the screen of the fir trees till he dropped into a luxurious open-air slumber.

As he slowly emerged from it, some half hour later, remaining in a blissful state of semi-consciousness for a few seconds, he became aware, in a vague sort of way, of a crooning little voice half chanting near him, very near him, only completely screened off by a thick holly-bush. He wondered as he listened. It seemed an odd thing to hear a child in the Wilderness singing,

> 'I know a bank whereon the wild thyme grows,
> Where oxlips and the nodding, nodding violet blows.'

Then a soliloquy. 'I wonder what sort of flowers oxlips are, but I'm afraid they come in spring. It's such a pity now that most of everything is gone over. I should like to find oxlips and violets.' Then again it broke into singing,

> 'There sleeps the fairy queen.'

Another pause, and a musing repetition. 'The fairy queen. This would be a nice place for fairies.'

Graham raised himself on his elbows

and tried to look through the leafy screen. At the same moment Trim, who had been dozing as well as his master, started up with a short bark and dashed through a hole in the bush. Graham heard a shrill cry, half-frightened, half-laughing. In a minute he skirted the holly bush, calling his dog and sending an assurance of Trim's good temper before him. He found Madge, with her crutch beside her, sitting on the mossy stump of a tree with such few flowers as she had collected between her fingers. She looked up at him with an effort to rise, which he prevented, and a tide of crimson blushes overflooded her serious, childish face.

'Oh, please,' she stammered, 'am I trespassing? I didn't see the board till after I got in. If I am, I'll go away.'

'No, no,' he cried earnestly, putting her back in her seat and dropping down on the grass near her. 'Never mind the board. No one but poachers need trouble about that. But how did you get in?'

He glanced at her crutch.

'Oh, quite easily,' she said, still blushing and turning her head away from him to hide it. 'I walked with Gwen to a cottage near here—our washerwoman's cottage—and while she talked to her I came in. I get about very well. I—I suppose it is *your* wood?'

'Yes; do you know who I am?'

'Oh, yes,' she answered, stealing a shy momentary glance at him; 'you are Mr Hyphen Graham, aren't you?'

Graham put his hand over his mouth to hide his smile. He always got on with children, chiefly because he took them seriously and never made them feel ridiculous.

'*Brooke*-Graham,' he answered lightly. 'Yes. And your are Miss Margaret Lane?'

'Yes; but they call me Madge.'

'May I call you Madge?'

'Certainly,' the child answered, with a pretty, quaint, little air of dignified courtesy.

'Do you like this place, Madge? I fancy you are not used to the country.'

'No. We have lived in London for a good while, and before that at

Boulogne, in France, you know. I have never been accustomed to the country, but I like it—im—mensely.'

'That is right. Then you will enjoy being here, I hope.'

'Yes. But it won't be for long—not for always. The real vicar will come back.'

'Should you like it to be for long?'

'Yes, of course, I should. It is not nice moving so often, but,' she added, with an old sort of sigh, 'people must put up with things. It is nice while it lasts.'

'How old are you, Madge?'

'Nearly eleven.'

'You talk sometimes as if you were a woman.'

She blushed.

'I am afraid I do. Ettie laughs at

me, and father. They say I am old-fashioned, but I can't help it if I am. I have not been able to see many children, and have not had anyone to play with. Jack and Sidney are next to me, and they are big boys at school. I was a twin. I wish the other twin had lived; it was a girl. It would have been nice.'

'It is rather lonely for you. Your sisters are so much older.'

'Yes. Gwen is twenty, and Ettie eighteen and a half. But Gwen is always good to me. Of course, she can't play games—at least she doesn't care to, much—but I can say what I like to her, and she reads to me, and when I am in pain she nurses me. I always sleep with Gwen.'

'I guess that you are very fond of her.'

'Oh, very, very fond!' the child cried fervently. Now that her first shyness was gone, she seemed to find it easy to talk to Graham, and to confide in his kind, clear grey eyes. 'People generally like Ettie best, but they don't know. Gwen is like mother; the boys and Ettie are different. Jack is good-natured, but I do not care much for Sid. I am afraid he will give a great deal of trouble.'

'Boys are often troublesome.'

'Yes. Jack is, too; he gets into scrapes, but Sid is rather bad. Most boys seem bad. Don't you think so?'

'Oh, I hope not. That is a little strong. I said troublesome. I know we are all of us that.'

'But the pupils father gets are bad, really bad often. I never have to do with them. Only one, he was of "weak intellect," that's what they said, but not bad, I liked him, and he was very fond of me. We played beggar my neighbour together, he never could learn cassino, I believe he is coming back, I shall be glad, but mother says it is a great trouble. I wish we need not have pupils, but we must for the money. We are very poor, you know.'

Graham felt half ashamed of listening to this innocent revelation of what probably the rest of Madge's family would not wish him to know, but he was interested. He wanted always to attach a meaning to, to account for, Gwen's sad looks. Madge did not paint a rose-coloured existence.

'I am sorry,' he said vaguely, looking down at Trim, who lay between his legs, and pulling a tangle out of his ear.

'Yes, it is not nice to be poor,' Madge said, sighing; 'but I suppose *you* don't know anything about it. Father says you must be very rich.'

Graham felt quite anxious to justify himself as from an accusation.

'I assure you I have been anything but rich; I know quite well what it means to be poor.'

'*Do you?*' Madge said wonderingly. 'Well, it isn't nice, is it? not to be able to buy anything, and, if one wants new frocks or boots, to have father angry and saying he hasn't got a brass farthing and he shall end in the workhouse. We don't believe *that* of course. There are not ladies and gentlemen in the workhouse; but we never have any money, and mother is unhappy about it.'

'I wonder if your mother would like your telling me,' Graham said gently. Madge blushed furiously, and her eyes filled. He felt as if he had struck her, and hastened to say, 'Don't mind, Madge! I'll not repeat a word. I didn't mean to vex you. Let us be friends, and then you can say just what you like.'

She could not speak. Her throat was swelling with a sob, but her eyes were fixed imploringly on his. He took her small thin hand and patted it in a brotherly fashion.

'Come, say we shall be friends!'

'You'll not tell anyone what I said,' she gasped out; 'not about father being angry, and the workhouse, they'd be so vexed.'

'No, no, *indeed* I won't.'

'Thank you.'

'And we'll be friends?'

'But you're so—so old—'

'I am a good deal older than you, but that's no reason against it. People can be friends if there are any amount of years between them. I hope you'll come and see me.'

'At your house?' she asked, with brightening looks.

'Yes. There's an old pony in my stables, a *very* old quiet pony. I was thinking you might perhaps like to borrow him sometimes. Should you?'

'Oh, I *should!*'

'Then I hope you will—often. I will call him your pony.'

'Mine—at your stables?'

'Yes, why not? His name is John

Bull. It isn't a pretty name, they call him Johnny, he used to draw Mr Graham's chair. And you and your sisters will come into the Wilderness whenever you like, won't you?'

'Thank you,' Madge said again. She had now recovered her dignity. 'You are *very* kind. Ettie doesn't care much for country walks; she likes the Oldfield road best. But Gwen and I do, only Gwen isn't quite sure it's safe. She is a little frightened about tramps and bulls.'

'There are never tramps or bulls in the Wilderness, it is quite near to my house.'

'I will tell her that. I often have to go alone, for there's plenty to do at home, especially when there are pupils.'

'Well, alone or with—with anybody—you'll be always welcome, Madge.'

She looked gratefully at him. To herself she said he was the very nicest man she knew, but she did not put this sentiment into words, only softly repeating her frequent 'Thank you.'

'I must go now, it must be tea-time I think, and Gwen will surely be ready. Good-bye, Mr—Mr—Brooke-Graham.'

'Stay, I'll help you to the entrance. It is rather rough walking. Should you mind if I lifted you over this bit?'

'No,' Madge said, though colouring, and he carried her to the edge of the plantation, leaving her on the other side of the park paling in the high road.

Madge limped away gaily, with the sensation of adoration which some girl children feel for young men springing warm within her, eager to tell Gwen of the delightful ways of Mr Brooke-Graham.

Graham went back towards home, thinking over the child's confidences, which had given him a good deal of insight into the ways of the Lane household, and some explanation of the melancholy looks that had been on his mind since he first saw Gwen and her mother. He thought he understood something of the clergyman's nature. He guessed him to be imprudent, ill-judging, hasty, and not too well principled, yet he felt disposed to be lenient and friendly. When a man is poor and out of luck it is not difficult to fall into ways which the more prudent and the prosperous find censurable. With a good balance at one's bankers, and an assured income, it is easy to win the chorus of approbation which attends the successful. He resolved to be a friend to the whole Lane family as well as to Madge. They interested him and roused his sympathy—never very dormant in Graham's breast. It would be pleasant to see Gwen look happy—very pleasant.

CHAPTER VI.

ERDLEY was not exactly a gay neighbourhood. The Miss Barnetts, on the contrary, declared it to be the 'very most hideously dull hole in Christendom;' but they were given to strong language and exaggerations, being, as Mrs Barnett said, 'so lively,' which liveliness showed itself chiefly in violent invective, or in raptures over 'dear fellows' and 'lovely dances.' But, on Mr Brooke-Graham's appearance in their midst, Erdley felt it ought to exert itself. The form of entertainment most popular, because the least expensive, was that 'cheap and

A Girl's Past.

nasty' one of garden-parties, but the advent of an eligible bachelor demanded more effort.

'Papa, we really must give a dinner for Mr Brooke-Graham,' Mrs Barnett protested.

'No, a dance!' implored the daughters.

Papa, however, who showed symptoms of yielding to the dinner, struck at the dance, and the girls had to give way, reflecting that after all it would be difficult to beat together young men enough to make it tolerable. The fast, objectionable, little Mrs Willard, who always got hold of men somehow, chose to have a dance however, so, almost simultaneously, Graham received Mrs Barnett's invitation to dine on the third of November, Mrs Willard's off-hand announcement of a 'carpet dance,' and two or three other requests for the pleasure of his company at dinner or at lunch, to the Willoughbys' and one or others. He accepted all with ready complacency.

'Shall you ask these Lanes?' Mrs Willard inquired of the second Miss Barnett, Charlotte, generally known as Chatty, the best-looking and the most advanced flirt of the four.

Mrs Willard threw a flavour of contempt into her tone. The Lanes did not seem to be going to be popular with the Erdley ladies.

'The mater says we must. Mr and Mrs and one Miss Lane. We can't do with two.'

'To a dance I must ask the lot. What do you think of them, Chatty?'

Chatty tossed her be-frizzled light head.

'Well, not much. They seem shady rather to me — and shabby. Such clothes! I wouldn't give sixpence for the whole turn-out.'

'Pretty, d'you think?' Mrs Willard asked casually, remarking to herself meanwhile how Chatty Barnett was ageing, and how red her nose got sometimes.

'Rather,' grudgingly. 'The dark one looks glum, and the other is not exactly good form, is she?'

An outsider would hardly have considered either of the two ladies who were thus conversing as the best judge of 'good form,' but people have not yet the 'giftie' to see themselves as others see them, and they agreed complacently as to poor Ettie not being 'much of it.' But the Lanes were bidden to the impending festivities.

Mrs Lane opened the two notes at breakfast. The Barnetts' card for the Rev. W., Mrs and Miss Lane, and the Willard's for the family. She looked half frightened as she read them.

'What have you there, mamma?' her husband asked in his sonorous, imperious, marital accents, stretching out his hand. He read them aloud. 'So! Invitations are pouring in,' he remarked with some gratification. 'We promise to be gay.'

'Must we accept?' Mrs Lane asked anxiously.

She longed for a loophole of escape. To her shy nervous temper and morbid consciousness of shabby clothes, company was a terror.

'Of course, of course,' her husband decided. 'You and I and one of the

A Girl's Past. 119

girls'—he glanced at Ettie—'to the Barnetts' dinner, you and the girls only to the dance.'

'I don't want to go,' Gwen said briefly.

Both Ettie and her father looked relieved.

'Well, we can make an excuse for you to the Barnetts. Only one is asked there. But it will look marked if you don't both go to this dance.'

'I have no proper clothes. I don't want.'

'Pooh, pooh! Buy some cheap fluffy stuff, and make it up at home. Anything will do for a small dance. As for the dinner, that's a little different—one must be decent. What have you, Esther? Only that eternal moiré? Could you make it respectable with black lace or something?'

Mr Lane was one of those domestic autocrats, frequently found amongst the clergy, who like to meddle and to rule, even in the purely feminine departments. He knew exactly the contents of his wife and daughters' wardrobes.

'Yes, oh yes,' she answered eagerly. 'It does not matter what I wear.'

'Not much,' he retorted, almost brutally. He was fond of his wife in a fitful, commonplace fashion, but he had a very poor opinion of her. 'But as for Ettie—Ettie should have a new frock.'

'I want one awfully,' Ettie put in, with sparkling eyes, and the radiance of hope flushing her pretty face.

A Girl's Past.

'Yes, you do, my poor pet,' he said, as tenderly as he was capable of speaking; 'and you must have your chances now you are young and pretty. Let me see.' He stroked his long whiskers with one small red hand contemplatively. 'That seems a decentish draper's—the churchwarden Phillips. Go there and choose something, not expensive—that soft sort of silk—what do they call it? Pongee, is it? I daresay the village dressmaker can manage if you give her ideas.'

'The third of November,' Mrs Lane said musingly. 'When is it the pupils come, William?'

'Not till the sixth. At least young Turvey on the sixth, Johnstone on the seventh. I shall go to Oldfield to meet Turvey, stop there a night, and bring them both on the seventh.'

Mrs Lane sighed heavily, a sound that always irritated her husband.

'I wish you wouldn't moan over things, Esther,' he said sharply. 'These fellows are a necessary evil. You needn't make so much of them. I wish you were not so given over to dismality. I am sure things are worse for me than you, but I keep up some spirit. I am not always groaning.'

Fortunately for him this was true. Foiled, unsuccessful, a hundred times at the lowest ebb of fortune, he had a certain sanguine elasticity which rebounded from the depths. He would occasionally yield to angry despair, often to violent rages at fortune, but he could always recover and keep a certain power of enjoyment. Mrs Lane had long ago accepted the defeat of life patiently, and had lost every hope with uncomplaining quietude, but though she was patient she could not help being depressed, and her depression always made her husband angry whenever it struck him forcibly.

'I don't mind poor Turvey,' she said, trying to put a little more cheerfulness into her voice; 'he is harmless and kind enough, but I own I am a little frightened by the idea of Johnstone.'

'Oh, he may be better than we think; at any rate his father is very liberal, and we need the money, Heaven knows. Well, I must go. Write and accept these invitations, Esther, and go to Phillips and see what you can do.'

'Am I to pay him?' Mrs Lane asked timidly.

'Oh, no; not till Christmas,' the clergyman returned airily. 'Don't run me up a big bill, but get what's necessary to make Ettie look respectable. Those Barnett girls are inclined to sneer, I can see, and I want my girl to outshine them and make them jealous of her good looks.'

He stooped to give Ettie a kiss as he passed, for which she put up her pretty rosy mouth. It was impossible to help noticing the marked difference he showed between his daughters.

Mrs Lane glanced at Gwen with a tender sort of apology, and put out a furtive hand to touch hers.

'You really don't want to go, Gwennie?' she said gently.

'No, of course not, mother,' the girl answered, in her low, level voice. 'I

A Girl's Past.   125

should hate it. I had much rather keep away from the dance.'

'Stuff, Gwen,' Ettie interrupted, in her father's very tones. 'It would look very bad. You *must* go. You can sit in a dark corner and be dreary there if you like. You're not obliged to *dance*.' She got up and gave a kind of pirouette. 'Oh, how jolly to think of parties and a new frock!'

Mrs Lane and Gwen smiled simultaneously as they looked at her; the same kind of maternal, sympathetic interest on both faces, though one was nearly as young as Ettie's.

'Come on, Gwen, to Phillips,' Ettie continued. 'Now that papa is so amenable we must really get a good many things. Oh, how I *love* buying. If I could marry a well-to-do man, and go out shopping with a fat, heavy purse, how *heavenly* it would feel.'

The shopping was to the purpose, and though the clergyman's wife looked dowdy enough at the Barnetts' dinner-party, the pretty daughter shone like a freshly-set jewel in her new silk frock. Her pinky-white, smooth neck and round arms gave an extra charm to her girlish, fair beauty. Gwen had dressed her hair most becomingly, and had lent her her own string of pearls.

The Miss Barnetts felt unchristian sentiments about her when they noticed Brooke-Graham's expression of admiring surprise. Ettie had a great appetite for pleasure, which had never yet been at all adequately satisfied. To dress, to look pretty, to attract, these were the ideals of her life. She had been starved or only half fed with them. How her eyes sparkled with expectant pleasure. Youth and gaiety gave her a new vivacity. She knew she looked her best, and was radiant in the knowledge. Yet though Graham's cool, grey eyes reflected some of the pleasure in hers, he was conscious of a distinct disappointment. Why was only 'the fair one' present? Where was the Lady of Shadow? There was Mr Lane, in respectable, ultra-clerical garb, brushed and spruce; his delicate features and reddened complexion and slightly bloodshot eyes a sort of elderly caricature of Ettie; his greyish, straggling, Dundreary whiskers and rather scraggy moustache were trimmed for the occasion. He smiled, bowed, and complimented, covering his wife's nervous timidity and feeble conversation with a flow of facile talk, 'not badly done, but a little too much of it,' as Mr Willoughby said. Some apology was made, or half made, for his eldest daughter.

Mrs Barnett hardly cared to listen. She took no interest (unless a slightly malign one) in the pretty sisters, and had carefully arranged to seat whichever of them came between two ineligibles, a boyish, bank-clerk asked to fill up a gap, and Mr Willoughby, who was afraid of young ladies, and particularly awkward with them.

Ettie, however, was never to be snubbed. She cultivated the baby bank-clerk, who soon rose to the occasion, put his diffidence into his pocket, began to giggle and make giggle, and was exceedingly happy in his juxtaposition to so pretty and agreeable a partner.

Graham found himself on the other side of the table, between Mrs Barnett and her daughter Chatty. He had been considered to prefer the second Miss Barnett, so her elder sister had loyally retired in her favour, and was stalking a less eligible, but more easily captured quarry in the shape of a widowed solicitor from Oldfield. Graham was polite, but he felt distinctly bored. Mrs Barnett had only two lines of conversation— gossip about her neighbours, praise of her own family. She was amusing in neither. Chatty tossed and prinked, shrugged her white shoulders, and made play with a pair of large light prominent blue eyes in vain. Graham was polite but irresponsive. She caught him once or twice looking with approval (she thought), at that 'little flirting, underbred Miss Lane,' and was as intensely indignant with her as if she herself had never flirted.

Vanity Fair—in a reduced and shabby form—may be held in the depths of the country; and girls who have no interests, no occupations, few scruples, and still fewer ideas, will make fools of themselves to the end of time.

After dinner Chatty had to give up even the appearance of monopolising Mr Brooke-Graham. He went to Ettie as soon as he entered the drawing-room, and took a vacant seat by her at once, regardless, or careless of the Miss Barnett's bitter glances.

Ettie looked up at him with her childish, dimpled smile, which he thought one of the nicest things about her. She might be a little coquette, but she was still fresh, young and naïve.

'Well,' he said, 'did you enjoy that long age of a dinner?'

'Oh, yes,' she said; 'didn't you?'

'First tell me why you did, and then I'll answer you.'

'Why? Oh, I don't know. I've been out so little, I suppose I'd enjoy *anything*. I like nice things to eat and drink,' she added, with a sly little look; 'champagne and iced pudding after cold water and cold mutton, *comme à l'ordinaire*. Then it's fun to see people, and—'

'And to flirt with a young fellow just initiated, eh?'

Even as he spoke, Graham was conscious that he would not have dreamt of speaking like this to Ettie's sister. Ettie did not mind; she laughed and nodded.

'Well, he's not a bad boy. Now tell me, Mr—Mr—must I always say *Brooke*-Graham, it is such a mouthful?'

'Oh, no, call me just what you please.'

'Well tell me, Mr Graham, then, why you *didn't* enjoy your dinner?'

She hoped, with mischief, that he would respond by running down Miss Chatty Barnett, whom Ettie already recognised as an enemy; but that was not Graham's way.

'Oh, I don't know,' he answered carelessly. 'It was long and hot, and I always find conventional big dinners rather a bore. Why isn't your sister here?'

'She did not care to come.'

'Does she dislike going out always?'

'I believe she does. Gwen is shy, you know. She says she has no company talk.'

'She is not so bright and merry as you.'

'No,' Ettie returned, with calm complacency. 'I always took things differently. I look at the bright side of things, fortunately for me, for they never are too bright with us.'

'And your sister is easily depressed?'

Ettie nodded.

'Does she *always* dislike going everywhere?' he asked, a little wistfully.

'Oh, I don't know,' Ettie said, with nonchalance.

She did not find it interesting to discuss Gwen.

'I want you all to come to *me* to some kind of a party. I was thinking if you'd lunch with me, all of you, Madge included, on Thursday.'

'On Thursday? let me see, that's the eighth. Father will be away. He is going to fetch some pupils. But that wouldn't matter,' she added naïvely; 'we could come. It would be awfully jolly.'

'Do you think so? I will ask your mother. Your father could have a bachelor's dinner with me some other time. I'll have Mrs Willoughby as hostess, but the party shall be yours; you shall arrange it.'

'Shall I? How jolly!' Ettie cried again with bright eyes. The girl of the period has a 'universal adjective' as well as the London rough. 'Shall I settle it?'

A Girl's Past.

'Yes, in every detail. You don't object to Mrs Willoughby?'

'No,' the girl admitted, condescendingly. 'She seems nice. Someone told me she had only been a little while married, but it can't be true.'

'Why not? It is, however. Brides are not *always* about twenty.'

'No, but she does look old.'

'Well, about my party—your party? You and your mother and sisters wiil come.'

'What a heap of undiluted womankind!'

'I must have you all four, particularly Madge. She and I are sworn friends.'

'Really? She's a queer, whimsical little mortal! Well, us four, who else? Mr and Mrs Willoughby. Please *not* the Barnetts nor the Willards!'

He laughed at her candour.

'Why not?'

'Oh, I don't like them, and they don't like me. You won't ask them?'

'I said you should have it all your own way.'

'How kind you are! Then who else?'

'Do you object to young Fairfax and Fred Ray? That will be quite enough. They both play tennis, and we can get up a set. Now, please,' getting out his notebook, 'what will you have for luncheon? "Which are your favourite vanities?" Champagne I know, iced pudding I know, What else?'

'Jugged hare,' she said, laughing, 'and *anything* with cream.'

He gravely put down these items, extracted a few more confessions, and promised to do his best.

'Look how that girl is throwing herself at his head!' Chatty Barnett whispered bitterly to her next sister. 'Disgusting, I call it! How silly men are! Any flirting, giggling minx can take them in if she's bold enough. Now he is wanting her to sing! Well *I* believe these Lanes are regular adventurers! The Coombs knew someone who knew a person that remembered to have heard something *very shady* about them. I hope ma won't encourage her showing off.'

Ettie did sing, and was much applauded. Chatty's cup of bitterness was full. Mr Brooke-Graham 'flirted with her,' as she chose to call it, all the evening, was very polite to poor, sad, inoffensive Mrs Lane, and secured her promise for herself and daughters on the eighth. Mr Lane congratulated himself, when alone with his wife, on Ettie's success.

'Graham's taken with her, there's no doubt of that, Esther. We may hope to see the little puss well settled one of these days, and if old Merryweather never recovers, who can tell? *We* might be comfortably settled at the Parsonage, and Miss Ettie Lady of the Manor; eh, my dear?'

'Things don't happen like that—to us,' Mrs Lane murmured. Fortunately for her Mr Lane did not hear the remark. He was building his usual castles in the air. He had quite a principality in those ethereal regions already,

CHAPTER VII.

GRAHAM was not disappointed again at the Willards' carpet dance by Gwen's non-appearance, yet he did not get much satisfaction from her presence. She kept resolutely in the background, and though she looked very nearly beautiful in her cloud of white, and would have looked quite so but for her reserve and pallor, she was not much noticed and sought after. Ettie quite outshone her, and was the belle of the night. Gwen did not dance waltzes, she said, they made her so dizzy — she had headaches after them. She refused him again and again, only dancing once in a lancers with him, and once or twice more with partners who seemed to find nothing to say to her, and whom she regarded with her sad indifferent eyes as she did most things. Only for a brief space she warmed and lighted up. When Graham talked about Madge the soft flitting smile and colour came for the moment, and her deep, dark eyes were illuminated with tenderness.

'She adores you, I think,' she said, looking up at him for a moment while the brightness and softening lasted, 'especially since you sent Johnny round for her. It was so kind of you. We went for a picnic. We got right to the top of Durrock

Hill. There was such a splendid view, Madge enjoyed herself immensely, the hill air gave her quite a colour.'

'Is she very delicate?'

'She is stronger than she was. She nearly died several times before she was seven. Now, except for her lameness, the doctors think she may grow up tolerably strong.'

'She is a dear little maid.'

'Yes.'

Gwen did not gush. She added nothing to the one full, deep monosyllable, but it came from her heart. He saw that she *could* love, and strongly too. Reserved as she was, he knew that she had no ordinary affection for this frail little sister.

'She is like you,' he said.

Gwen darted at him a look curiously mixed of terror and anger.

'Oh, no, she is not! oh, I *hope* not—'

She paused, struck suddenly by his look of astonishment at her reception of this seemingly innocent remark, and tried hard to force out an odd, cold little laugh, as if to convince him she had meant nothing by her words.

'You *hope* not?' he repeated.

'Well,' she said, in an embarassed way, looking in an opposite direction from him, 'I mean—if I meant anything —I had rather she struck out a new line.'

'For my part I like Madge all the better for the likeness,' he said, rather under his breath.

She either did not or would not hear, changing the subject abruptly.

A Girl's Past. 143

'I was wondering,' she said brusquely, 'whether Mrs Willard is what people call pretty?'

'Some men think so,' he answered, indifferently; 'she is not my style. Is she yours?'

'No. She is—she looks so bold, so self-conscious. But I daresay,' she added quickly, 'it is only her looks; she may be very nice.'

He had noticed in Gwen before an odd reluctance to speak ill of people, especially of her own sex. Unlike Ettie, who vituperated freely such people as she declared she 'hated' and 'abhorred' with all the frank intolerance and vehemence of youth, Gwen had generally some saving clause, and scarcely ever committed herself to a violently inimical statement. On the other hand she made no friends. She was cold, shy, reserved, unresponsive to all. A poor, kind, invalided old maid whom she visited and did little ministrations to, and Mrs Willoughby, whose gentle courtesy seemed to attract her, were the only slight exceptions. No man could light a ray in her dark, sombre eyes. She had no sweet looks, no wreathèd smiles for the gay Lotharios of the county.

Graham had an odd persistency in dwelling on an idea, a great power of absorbing himself in a subject, an interest.

Gweneth Lane had first attracted him, and now bade fair to occupy a large part of his thoughts. She puzzled him, she was a problem. From his schoolboy days he had liked to fasten his wits to a puzzle, he began to be

A Girl's Past.

in desperate earnest about solving this one. Her relations with her family and neighbours seemed peculiar, she stood alone. Between her mother and herself he could divine signs of a deep and genuine affection; they watched each other with solicitous interest, each seemed anxious to spare, to serve the other. Yet even here, he fancied, there was not actual intimacy or unreserve. Her next sister and she were not much together; there were none of the signs of confidence, of comradeship between them that often exists between sisters. They did not quarrel, but they went different ways; no whispers, signs, or any of the freemasonry of close relationship were to be observed.

And there were positive signs of a more decided antagonism in Mr Lane's manner and bearing with his eldest daughter. He had acquired a suave mannerism in society, partly clerical, partly conventional, which led him to adopt an artificial blandness towards her when it was necessary, but of the open, kindly, paternal, there was not a trace. Under the smooth manner Graham even thought he detected dislike, or, at least, a sort of animosity, strikingly in contrast with his obvious, unstudied, palpable admiration and fondness for his daughter Esther.

With Madge, and Madge alone, Gwen seemed like other girls—natural, affectionate, and at ease. Her face, with its unconscious pathos, repressed, yet impossible to disguise, the lonely, fixed unyouthful sadness which dwelt in the depths of her eyes, pressed on his

A Girl's Past. 147

heart with an insistent, almost a painful claim.

He longed to find out that it was but a trick — a habit of countenance, to discover some girlish enjoyment of things, some unreasoning gaiety in her, to be able to draw smiles — genuine smiles, not the faint attempts which were as inadequate as sunshine through mist—to her lips, to hear her laugh out loud, to see her behave in some foolish, lively, youthful fashion, which would relieve him of some of the tiresome pain of pity—pity which had no ground in fact, as far as he knew. What was there exceptionally miserable in her condition, even if it were not the brightest lot in the world? True, the Lanes were poor, even very poor, this was evident enough. True, they seemed to have led a somewhat unlucky kind of existence. The boys, of whose sins Madge had so frankly told him, were very likely a trouble and anxiety. The pupils—to take the same small philosopher's judgment of them—were apparently unpleasant inmates to endure, but need she be unhappy for these causes? Ettie had the same obstacles to enjoyment of life, but Ettie was gay as a lark! Had she been crossed in love? Possibly. Had she perhaps lost by death or separation someone dearer than the rest of the world? It might be so. Meanwhile she remained a mystery—a riddle—to the solution of which he bent his resolute and obstinate mind. He tried hard to get her to like him—to be friendly and confidential. It was a difficult task,

A Girl's Past. 149

yet he fancied he won some slight measure of success. He fancied, at any rate, she had no dislike for him. She would not talk much, but her glance dwelt on him once or twice with an indefinite kind of softness. She seemed to look on his face as that of one friendly to her, and as if she wondered why he were so. He might, perhaps, be justly said to 'flirt' with Ettie—that is to say, he allowed himself to be flirted with; he laughed, talked, chaffed and danced with her, he paid her openly candid compliments, they were already on a tolerably intimate footing. With Gwen there was not the faintest approach to anything of this sort. Yet Graham was really not conceited or coxcombical with Ettie; he did not imagine there was a scrap of real earnest under the rather rollicking levity of the astute young person who seemed perfectly able to guard her own heart and peace, whose bright, hard, blue eyes neither melted nor sank beneath his, who was evidently only bent on the enjoyment of the moment — at least this was the view he took. He had too newly attained what Kitty called his 'principality,' to understand that he had become an object for the ambitious and worldly hopes of marriageable young ladies. He did not realise Ettie's hard stratum of common sense and purpose of self-aggrandisement under the light, gay froth on the surface. She was not, he was sure, in danger of being in love with him, and he had a certain simple chivalry in him which forbade his comprehension of a possibility of so young a girl falling in love with a place and an income. He thought a great deal more of one look from Gwen's serious deep eyes than of a thousand wiles and smiles from the pretty, fair Ettie. He enjoyed the Willards' dance, though it gave him but a meagre allowance of Gwen's society, much more than the Barnetts' state dinner, and he intended to get considerably more satisfaction still out of his own lunch-party.

The morning of this latter event was one of the last days of the second summer they were enjoying, with just enough of crispness in the warmth to exhilarate the spirits. Even Gwen felt a glow of cheerful girlish hope and pleasure as she came down to a late breakfast, at which Mr Lane was not present. He had left early on his pupil-catching expedition. This fact alone, that for a day or two her father would be out of the way, was a gain. It was shocking, of course, that it should be so, Gwen would have shrunk from saying so much in words, yet she knew in her heart that she breathed more freely, felt more cheerful, without the possibility of meeting her father's brief, unfriendly glance, or hearing his voice, either raised in irritable reproach or bitter with disapproval. She did not mean to be unfilial, but she could not love him, and she felt in every nerve of her conscious being that he had no affection for her.

Besides, it was a bracing, delicious autumn day, she was not twenty-one, and she was going to a place where she expected to enjoy herself. All

A Girl's Past. 153

these reasons combined to give a certain sweetness to her sensations, which was rare enough. She spoke more than usual, and with more animation. Her pale, careworn mother smiled with pleasure. Ettie was not apt to be low-spirited at any time, and was exultant with her own successes and hopes. Madge was delighted to be asked 'with the grown-ups' by her dear Mr Brooke-Graham, so the meagre breakfast was a much more festal meal than usual. It was even, in its poor way, a secret satisfaction to the anxious matron to be spared ordering any dinner. The butcher's bills were never off her mind, and wherever she went they rose upon her like spectres, her life was one long struggle with griping poverty. No wonder her poor forehead was furrowed, her poor lips pinched and drawn down at the corners. These were the scars of her constant and ignoble battle. She looked for nothing else from life, till these, and all other cares, could be laid down by the side of the grave. Her only hope was that the girls might escape such a lot, her only constant satisfaction that her husband did not 'take things' as she did, and managed, somehow or other, to get more pleasure out of his life than could easily have been imagined. She loved him, he had been, on the whole, a kind husband to her, yet she owned him 'trying,' and could not but admit to herself that it was a certain relief to have him absent for any length of time. Yet with that unconscious hypocrisy which timid, gentle women learn as a second nature, she tried a faint regret that 'your poor dear papa' should lose this party. No one, not even his favourite daughter, cared to join in this sentiment.

Mr Brooke-Graham had not forgotten any of Miss Ettie's pet 'vanities'; the hospitable lunch-table was crowded with good things and sweet things. Mrs Willoughby's feminine taste had a little curtailed and chastened the superabundance of his bachelor providings, but enough was left to have furnished a luxurious meal to twenty guests instead of half-a-dozen. Ettie did full justice to his thoughtful remembrance of her taste, and ate a very hearty and satisfactory meal. Madge seemed also to be indulging herself in unwonted gluttony to her anxious shy mother, to whom poverty had taught a rather uncomfortable habit of watching the appetites of her children. She was a little shocked at what seemed to her almost like excess, and ventured a feeble remonstrance when Graham would insist in pressing fresh supplies of delicacies on the blushing little girl, whose pleading eyes seemed to implore her mother for once to overlook the extraordinary feasting. Gwen ate as little as a bird. She had long ago learnt to curb the inconvenient appetite of a growing girl, and to 'go without,' and the habit had become nature. The joys of the senses did not appear to be evident to her. It was all Graham could do to get her to drink one small glass of champagne, while Ettie took two or three with the careless freedom of another and an altogether different nature.

A Girl's Past.

It was her gay soprano that made the most noise at the luncheon-table. Gwen's low-spoken few sentences came only now and then in answer to Mrs Willoughby's kind polite questions, or when Graham made an effort to bring her into the conversation. After lunch, when he came into the drawing-room to join his visitors in taking coffee, he found Gwen by herself in one window, apart from the rest, who were looking at some of old Mr Graham's *bric-à-brac* at the other end of the room. Gwen was rather listlessly turning over Graham's bachelor photograph album. He joined her and sat so as to keep her, as it were, almost imprisoned in her little recess. There were chiefly men in the book. Graham was not, and had never, been, a 'ladies' man.' Beyond portraits of his mother and sister, and of one or two celebrities, nearly all were of school and college friends, or chums met abroad. Gwen turned over the pages rather mechanically as Graham made a short running catalogue of names. Suddenly she paused at one page, and he heard her draw in her breath hard. She looked at him involuntarily, with a question in her eyes. She was very pale, some curious surprise or emotion contracted her mouth. He glanced at the photograph which lay open before them.

'Do you know him? That's a fellow I met in India somewhere. I did not know him well. I believe I've forgotten his name—Hollington, was it? No—something like that—let me see.'

But Gwen had quickly turned on;

she was evidently struggling to show no confusion.

'No, I was mistaken. It was very like someone I—we—knew—a pupil of father's. It startled me—a little—it was so like.' She hurried on with unusual volubility. 'This is your sister again, of course. What a nice picture! She is very pretty.'

'No, she is not really, not *very* pretty. That is a flattering presentment, smoothed and toned down as they do photographs now. She is nice-looking, and a jolly little thing. Some day, Miss Lane, I hope you will know her—and be friends.'

She shook her head with an odd, uncheerful smile.

'What do you mean by that? by shaking your head,' he asked, a little indignantly. 'Why should not you make friends with my sister?'

'She would not like me—I do not make friends.'

'What nonsense,' he said bluntly. 'I beg your pardon, I can give it no other name.'

'It is not nonsense, it is true,' the low, sad voice protested. 'I *cannot*. Girls could not like me.'

'And why not?'

'I—I am not agreeable. I do not know how to begin.'

'You cannot judge of yourself; you are unfair, you fancy things.'

'Oh, but one *can* judge of oneself better than others, for one *knows*. Indeed, Mr Graham, I am not saying this to make you compliment me.'

She said these words with an innocent,

A Girl's Past. 161

wistful candour that reminded him of Madge. She looked at him earnestly, without a spark of coquettish allurement. The words and tone touched him in an indescribable way. She seemed, as she spoke, so young, so sincere, with a sweetness in her sudden lapse into confidence he had never seen in her face before.

'You must let me go on believing I know you,' he said, dropping his voice with a sudden deepening of tone, which an experienced woman knows the meaning of. 'Without trying to pay compliments, you must let me say that I am sure my way of thinking of you is truer than your own. You have a bad habit of self-depreciation. If Kitty agrees with me, as she often does, you and she *will* be friends.'

Again she shook her head, but a

faint colour and a half-reluctant smile followed.

'I am afraid not. I am afraid I know too well that you are only saying that to be kind. Ettie makes friends *easily*, I never do.'

'Perhaps you have not had many chances.'

'No, I have not. We have never stayed long enough in places for me to get used to people, and I am stupidly afraid of everybody.'

'I hope you will stay here long enough to be understood and to understand.'

She seemed suddenly to draw back. The 'good moment' was gone, and the brief spell of unreserve. It was evident she would speak no longer of herself. He had noticed before how

A Girl's Past.   163

she shied from intimate talk, or any sort of self-revealing, like a timid horse. He got no more half-confidences, no more *tête-à-têtes* with Gwen. They all went into the garden, and a game of tennis followed, in which Ettie played (very badly).

Gwen would not even attempt to learn. 'It spoils the set,' she said, obstinately unpersuadable, and would hear no arguments in favour of making a beginning.

Ettie had no compunction about spoiling anyone's play. She sprang after every ball with excited little screams, and invariable non-success, and reduced the other players to inward maledictions, while they hypocritically pretended that it was rather nice than otherwise to have their play ruined by so pretty and vivacious a little spoilsport.

Mr Willoughby, who was a good tennis-player, and liked the 'severity of the game' preserved, indulged in strong language apart to Graham, after being ignominiously beaten from no fault of his own.

'The girl's an impertinent little ape,' he declared. 'Why doesn't she practise in private before she destroys everyone's play in public? A chattering, forward minx!'

'Oh, poor child, you are too hard on her!' Graham responded, with the indulgence of youthful humanity to a pretty girl. 'She has had no chances.'

'The other one, though she is as much too cold and reserved as the other is forward, has twice her sense and twice her good looks,' Mr Willoughby declared. 'She knows when to keep quiet.'

'She certainly does,' Graham said rather ruefully—words which his friend took as bearing a reproach.

'Well,' he rejoined quickly, 'anything is better than chattering and showing off like that little fool.'

'She has not had the best schooling, I expect.'

'You mean she has a pretty face, which covers a multitude of sins,' Mr Willoughby returned grimly, and said no more.

Graham went straight to Gwen's quiet corner and asked her and Madge to come with him to investigate a certain jargonelle pear-tree, which bore a fine crop of sweet, yellow fruit.

In the orchard, picking up and eating the pears which Graham shook on to the grass, Gwen was suddenly surprised into being frank, free, and girlishly merry. She seemed to catch Madge's confidential friendliness, and to regard the clear-eyed, kind-voiced, young squire with candid confidence. She was a new and a fascinating Gwen in this aspect, running with outspread hands to catch the pears as they fell, juicy and luscious, into her brown, slender palms, biting them with her strong, small, white teeth with the zest of a child. For the moment the cloud was lifted. She looked, and was, happy. It was not even a great drawback to her pleasure when a wasp, that had hidden in the heart of a pear, crept out and stung her hand. The pang was more than made up for by Graham's anxious and tender solicitude. It was so new and sweet to be cared for with such eager sincerity. The pain that hurts is that which no one pities—the secret gnawing of an unshared anguish. Gwen had known that pain. She had no self-pity left when others were compassionate and kind. It had been to her, indeed, a halcyon day; she always kept its memory green.

That night when Madge, as she often did, started out of a bad dream with a cry, she found Gwen sitting by the window in the moonlight, with her chin on her clasped hands, as still as if she had fallen asleep. As the terror flitted, with her awakening to find herself not alone, Madge fell back on her pillow and looked at her sister

How still she sat. How pure and delicate the pale outline of her profile showed against the moonlit window.

'Gwen, dear,' she said at last, and the girl turned quickly towards her. 'Gwennie, what are you thinking about?'

'About to-day,' Gwen answered briefly.

'Wasn't it lovely? You *did* enjoy yourself, Gwennie dear?'

'Yes, I did.'

'And he *is* nice, isn't he?'

Gwen faintly smiled.

'Who is *he*, Madge?'

'Why, my Mr Graham, of course. You really like him?'

There was a moment's silence, then Madge thought she heard a low 'Yes,' too faint to satisfy her.

'Really, truly, Gwen? You *must* like him. He is so good and dear.'

'Oh, yes, yes. I like him. Go to sleep!'

Madge turned on her side half angrily. Why need Gwen speak so impatiently? She had not expected an enthusiastic answer.

CHAPTER VIII.

IN a place like Erdley, people need indeed be white as snow to escape detraction, and the new clergyman, who had taken Mr Merryweather's duty there, might, perhaps, be described as rather more neutral-tinted than unspotted in reputation. Some tales of extravagance, of imprudence, even hints of certain unclerical proclivities a little more reprehensible, had followed his track, and Erdley gossips began to shake their heads, and morally smack their lips, over stories not to his credit. He was by no means a good payer. The Erdley

A Girl's Past. 171

tradespeople were most yielding in the way of long-drawn accounts and almost unlimited credit, but when a man is stingy in his orders, and long-winded in his payments, the butcher and baker will begin to complain. He was plausible; he was very good in the church; he was attentive to the duties connected with it and occasionally kind to the sick and sorrowful, but a vague reputation began to float about him, fostered warmly by such ladies as were jealous of his daughters' beauty and Ettie's flirtations. They '*hoped* he did not drink;' but— 'his nose was red,' he was extraordinarily voluble sometimes, — Mr Willard had joked about a certain club dinner, when he showed the 'parson' home. Gale of the King's Head spoke of an order for spirits—if Mr Lane did not drink himself, those 'wretched pupils of his' did. The two youths he brought back with him to the Vicarage soon gave endless food to the scandal-mongers. Graham encountered them often in the village, and when he paid a rare visit to the public billiard-room. He recognised one by the description Madge had given of him as of 'weak intellect.' A tall, weedy creature, with weak eyes and a weaker smile, whose forehead and chin ran, as if frightened, away from the big nose, who twisted and cracked his red, knuckly fingers—this was the pupil generally called 'poor young Turvey.' His schoolfellows, of course, had called him 'Topsy-Turvey,' which was painfully descriptive of the state of his wits. He, at least, was harmless enough, except when some stronger and baser

A Girl's Past. 173

mind than his own coerced him, but the other specimen was far worse. A certain Bob Johnstone, a fellow tolerably well-born, and with plenty of money to come, who was destined by the doom of hereditary inclination to 'go to the bad.' Turvey, unfortunately for him, seemed to be a good deal under the influence of this hopeful youth, whose conversation, even in the presence of ladies, was far from refined, and in the company of men only was thickly larded with oaths and coarse expressions; and both of them appeared to be but vaguely supervised by their nominal preceptor, who did not evidently intend to spend very much of his time in a hopeless struggle to put learning into them and bad habits out. Their hours of study were certainly short enough, for they were constantly to be seen, the one swaggering, the other shambling about the place, smoking, frequenting the billiard-room, and the bar of the King's Head.

'Pupils indeed!' cried Mrs Barnett to Mrs Willard; 'a fine sort of a tutor Mr Lane makes them! He must advertise for refractory youths that everybody has given up as hopeless. Why, he lets them behave as disgracefully as they please. Our groom told Mr Barnett that Johnstone young man has been drunk ever so many nights. The other's only an idiot, and more to be pitied than blamed. Nice associates for a clergyman's wife and daughters! Any respectable man had rather break stones for a living than take such creatures into his own family.'

A Girl's Past.

Mrs Willard did not suggest, as she might have done, that an educated clergyman of small build and weak muscles would not make much by breaking stones. She agreed with Mrs Barnett that the Lanes were a 'queer lot,' and she, for her part, had not much opinion of any of them. She thought Mr Lane probably drank himself. Mrs Lane was a poor creature, very dull and difficult to get on with, while the girls—well, *Gweneth* gave her the idea of being somehow 'under a cloud,' and Ettie was the sort of girl to run away with a village blacksmith if she couldn't get a better husband by hook or by crook. Such kind and charitable expressions of opinion were not rare in Erdley, any more than in other small country places. However, even scandal herself hardly painted Mr Bob Johnstone blacker than he proved.

Graham had had various small collisions with him at the billiard-room, and on those afternoons, when he happened to meet him when he called (as he often did) on the Lanes. He hated him with the contemptuous disgust for all foul and unpleasant things which his clean, strong, healthy nature invariably felt. A longing desire to kick the fellow possessed him, which opportunity gave him the means of gratifying at last, one day about a month after the appearance of the 'pupils' on the scene. He was crossing the Wilderness, which made a short cut from the house to one part of the high road, when he heard voices near him amongst the bushes. One, Gwen's low contralto he was sure, though raised to a pitch he had never heard. It trembled, yet was loud with some tempest of fear or anger. He could not distinguish actually what she said, but he was sure that she spoke with some strong passion, and he heard following the insolent laugh and thick accents of the refractory pupil; and these words he could just catch as he neared them, 'Really, Miss Gwen, *you* need not be so stand off. Why can't you be decent to a fellow? You haven't always been so chary.' Here the voice sank and thickened into low, coarse accents, followed again by the insulting laugh of a half-drunken young blackguard. Then Graham heard again, 'It wouldn't kill you to give me a kiss. What's a kiss?' There was a sound of struggle, of rending bushes, and Gwen broke through the underwood, panting, crimson, with bright dilated eyes. She almost fell into Graham's arms. He was too enraged to stop for civilities. 'Where is he?' he said, in short, stern tones, pale with wrath. 'Where is the brute? Let me get at him.' Johnstone was not far off. He had struggled to follow Gwen, but, being more than half-drunk, had stumbled over a briar and lay full length at Graham's feet. The young squire kicked him as if he were an unclean beast.

'Get up,' he said. 'Be out of this! If you were sober I'd flog you. As it is, you ask Miss Lane's pardon when you have your senses, or I'll horsewhip you in public. Be off, this is *my* property! I don't allow drunken young blackguards about.'

Bob Johnstone struggled slowly into

a sitting posture, where he remained stupidly staring at the tall, strong figure that towered over him. He looked infinitely foolish, but almost as disgraceful. 'Get up! Be off!' Graham repeated, in tones Gwen had not believed his calm, kind voice capable of. 'I'll see Mr Lane to-morrow.'

The insolent stage was merging into the maudlin. The young reprobate got on to his feet with difficulty, and proceeded to protest that he meant no harm—only a 'mere flirtation'; that Mr Brooke-Graham was 'a damned sight too hard on a poor fellow that meant nothin';' as for being drunk, he swore by all his gods he was as sober—'as sober as—as you are.' As for insulting Miss Gwen, he thought far too much of her. He should never have stayed at 'old Lane's' if it hadn't been for 'the young ladies.' 'All the fellers fall in love with 'em,' he added, with a particularly loathly wink, which filled up the measure of Graham's wrath.

'Since you won't clear out of yourself, allow me to show you the way,' he said, with grim sarcasm, and, taking a grip of the starchless collar, he conducted Mr Johnstone to the road and started him, protesting against 'ungen'lemanly violence,' on his homeward way. Then he returned more slowly, making a considerable effort so to swallow his passion as to appear pretty much as usual before Gwen. She faced him with a desperate, quivering attempt at a smile. She could not force herself to be anything but pale —paler even than her wont—and her voice, as she desperately tried to make it sound unconcerned, had a sobbing cadence in it; yet it was evident she intended to let the incident go by.

'Please — please, Mr Graham,' she cried, even compelling herself to utter a little unreal short laugh, 'please don't make too much of this—this stupid rudeness of—of—that boy's. I daresay he— he meant nothing. You'll not let it go any further? You'll not say anything to —to my father?'

Graham looked at her in grave, surprised displeasure. He was longing for the time and chance of humbling and punishing the disreputable young cad who had insulted Gwen, and made her —for the moment when she broke through the bushes — look so tragical, so scornful and so beautiful all at once. Her eager desire now to hush it up, to soften his wrath, was repellent to him. Why should she care about the further issue of his righteous disgust? Why should she want to protect the young wretch?

'I was under the impression he needed a lesson in manners,' he said coldly. 'It would give me some pleasure to give him one.'

'I'd rather — much rather, you let it alone now,' she said quickly and nervously, not looking at him. A moment after she raised her eyes, and met his grave, curious look. She blushed all over her face, and her mouth trembled.

'You see,' she began again more quickly, more nervously, with an imploring pathos in her deep, sad eyes, 'we can't get rid of him yet. It would only be another bother—another upset at home—we—we are very poor. Poor people have to put up with all kinds of disagreeable things. I—I am very much obliged to you for interfering—he was very rude—I was annoyed, but —well, I know it is no excuse—but he had been drinking or he would not have behaved so. He is generally civil and keeps his distance. I can generally manage to protect myself.'

He was no longer angry, he was only vaguely pained and hurt for her.

'Gwen,' he said impetuously, and both were too strongly moved to notice till afterwards how he had addressed her, 'I can't bear to think that you should be exposed to the chance of being spoken to in that way—should have that disgusting young blackguard within reach of you. Could—can nothing be done with him?'

'He shall beg my pardon when he is sober,' Gwen said, with a faint smile. 'I sometimes can manage him better than the rest. Yes, I know he is horrid, but—we can't very well get rid of him. Father has undertaken to have him for a year.'

'For a year! It is contamination for you and your sisters.'

Graham was frowning again, at Fate, at Mr Lane, at the pupils, at anybody and everybody except Gwen.

'*Do* let me have it out with him,' he added, with a sudden boyish frankness which was very engaging.

Gwen shook her head, but her eyes were soft.

'No, no,' she said. 'Why should

you care? I—we are used, I am afraid, to that sort of contamination. We have always been too poor to be fastidious. Don't think about it any more, please, Mr Graham.'

'But I must — I can't help it — I must think about it, for it concerns you.'

'Not very deeply,' she said, with that faint smile again. 'Young Johnstone, after all, does not make much difference to my life. It is not at any time so very—' she stopped abruptly, coloured deeply, and began to move downwards towards the road.

'What were you going to say?'

'Oh, nothing—nothing. You must forget this, Mr Graham, you must really! It is not worth a second thought. If I ask you I know you will be kind enough not to make any more of it.'

'Then I am not to kick him? not to give him a thrashing?'

'Please not,' she said earnestly. 'It would make everything much worse.'

'Then of course I will not. Of course I will do what you really wish. You shall never have to ask me anything twice.'

'You are very kind to me,' she said, in a faltering voice, stooping to clear some clinging tendrils from her way. He stooped too, and in moving them touched her hand. She took it away quickly and hurried forward.

'Where are you going?' he asked. 'May I walk with you?'

'I am going to practise some new chants on the organ,' she said. 'Billy

Melhuish will be waiting at the church to blow the organ for me. I had better not take you out of your way.'

'My way is no way. I was only loafing. Do let me come into the church with you. It is a quiet, dreamy, little place. I love to sit in an empty church as the dusk comes on. The very spirit of silence and peace, the ghosts of a bygone past seem to fill it. If I should not be troublesome to you, I should like to hear you play.'

She said nothing, either of consent or denial. One voice within her urged her to send him away, another, more persistent, pleaded for one sweet reposeful hour in the weariness of the days. Brooke-Graham was her friend. She had not many, and the very scarcity made her prize those she had more than happier, richer girls do. She let him open the heavy, low-browed door for her, to light the candles by the organ, and to set the urchin going at the bellows. Then he sat on one of the singers' benches close behind her, and she began to play. The echoes in the empty little church rolled back the sweet, sonorous tones. Gwen began rather feebly, but the spirit of music came into her fingers after a few minutes, and she played her best for her one auditor, for Billy was but a mere stupid machine, who neither listened nor cared.

She tried over a couple of chants, and then, after pausing a moment, began softly and sweetly some of the tenderest bits from the 'Messiah'; not the triumphant choruses, but the plaintive suggestions of consolation in the midst of the sorrows and wrongs of the world, which appeal to the universal needs of man's inner self —'He shall feed his flock,' 'How beautiful are the feet.' Graham sat spellbound, in a profound quiescence. The music, the dimness, the sudden sinking into calm of his own angry emotions, all seemed to possess his soul with a deep overmastering sensation which he had neither power nor will to analyse. He only knew it was one of the supreme moments of life, which change the current of things.

At last the music suddenly stopped, from a very prosaic cause. Billy's time was up. He had to be home at five, and no music, however enthralling to educated minds, had power to win his rugged breast from thoughts of tea.

'Shall I blow for you? Do you wish to

go on playing?' Graham asked in a subdued voice, as she turned on her bench and told Billy he could leave.

'Oh, no,' she said, 'I must go too—they will want me, I daresay.'

But she did not immediately get up, and he sat down near her. He longed to lengthen out the dim sweetness of the hour, and she was loath to break the spell of rest which had fallen upon her from the place and the music.

'I wish—' he began softly, and then paused a moment. Then, as she started a little and looked at him, he went on: 'I wish you would tell me—you know we have made a compact of friendship, you and Madge and I — I wish you would tell me whether there is nothing at all I could do for you. When one has friends, you know, one is anxious to show that it is so, and I cannot help fancying—you must forgive me if it seems impertinent to say it—I cannot help fancying you are not quite happy somehow at home.'

'No, I am not,' she said under her breath; 'you are right. I am not at all happy.'

'Do you mind telling me why?' he said, in the softest, most coaxing of voices, just as he would have spoken to a child that was hurt.

'We—we are in church,' she said, with a startled little movement, a slight withdrawing from him. They were the first words that occurred to her, a vague protection from the seducing softness that made her long to pour out her heart, while all the instincts of the long habit of reserve resisted.

'Well,' he said half smiling, 'I am not saying or thinking anything that is profane. Surely one may care for people—one may wish to help—one's friends—in church?'

'I know you *are* my friend,' the words came reluctantly yet softly, 'and I have not many. I know you are very kind, but I—I am afraid I cannot tell you.'

'Will you let me say what I imagine makes you sad?'

'Oh, you—you cannot know, you cannot guess!' she cried, starting suddenly as if stung.

'Well, I have noticed — I have thought a great deal. I do often think about you. Just let me say one or two things. You have told me you have not many friends, you are very reserved and distant, which keeps people away, yet you don't like isolation, you are very sensitive and tender, it would make you happier to be liked.'

'I am afraid not. I can't be cordial and nice to people. I don't expect anyone to like me.'

'You fancy so, yet I believe I am right. If only you would trust more, be less reserved.'

'I cannot,' she said sadly. 'I have made up my mind to do without friends. I have mother and Madge.'

'But it is not natural, not right for a girl like you! You *ought not* to be so.'

'I know girls are expected to be bright and charming, to please and be pleased, but I am not like other girls. My life has been—has been full of trouble.'

'And you are only twenty!' he half-smiled, yet her words were a weight on his heart.

'People can be unhappy at twenty, at ten, at fifteen, at any age,' she said, with an undertone of passion. '*I* have never been anything else.'

'Gwen,' he said, in a voice of strong, manly reproach, 'you cannot mean what you say. You exaggerate—it cannot be so.'

'It is true,' she persisted, suddenly dropping her reserve and speaking strongly and fervently from her heart. 'I tell you it is true. There is too much said of the joys of childhood, I never had any, mine was a wretched, careworn childhood. I lay awake when I was little because I was too full of trouble to sleep. I woke to heavy, dreary thoughts.'

'Ettie is your sister, she did not suffer so.'

'Ettie and I are a whole world apart. She was born light-hearted and hopeful, things do not prey on her. I was born to be sorrowful, and I am sure I shall fulfil my destiny; in little things, and in great I am unlucky, and my nature is my worst misfortune. My mother was very unhappy before and after my birth. I never had a chance of being anything else.'

'It is very wrong to talk so. You are so young.'

'My body is young; my *self* feels old, very old, quite worn out and weary.'

He leant towards her, and stretched out his warm, strong, right hand.

'Dear, you must not talk so. Life

is before you. It shall be sweet yet. You must let me help you. I cannot bear to hear you speak so.'

She did not put her hand into his, though it sought eagerly to clasp it. She rose hastily, upsetting a whole pile of music books, which she stooped to pick up. A flurry of haste and bustle to be gone seemed suddenly to possess her.

'I had no idea how late it was. Please lock up the organ, Mr Graham. Is it light enough to see when the candles are out? Perhaps you can use one of those wax spills. Oh, thank you; I have the books all right. I must run home.'

'You'll let me go with you?'

'Oh, no,'—with a nervous, little laugh—'it is such a step of a way.

A Girl's Past. 197

No, I had rather not. If you will lock the church door, please, and leave the key at the cottage, I shall be obliged. Good-night, Mr Graham, good-night.' She hurried off, leaving him behind, but when he had locked the door he found her waiting to say a hurried, panting sentence. 'Mr Graham, just one word, please. I want you to forget everything, really *everything*, that has passed this afternoon. I have been talking nonsense. It is that you must forget, as well as that horrid boy's rudeness—everything.'

'I will do all I can for you,' he answered quietly, 'but if you ask me what is impossible I can make no promises. At least, you will allow that we are friends? *That* is not nonsense, not to be forgotten?'

'Oh, I *do* want a friend,' she said impetuously, then shrank from her own words. 'It depends on what it means, but thank you for all your kindness.'

'It is not *kindness*,' he cried, taking both her hands and holding them tight.

She wrenched them away.

'Oh, hush, that's nonsense,' she cried, in a forced, unnatural voice; 'it is just that and nothing else. You are very kind, and I am ever so much obliged to you. Good-night. I must make haste.'

She ran off, into the grey mist of the gathering evening, as if pursued. He stood and watched the slender, running figure till it was swallowed up in darkness. Then he turned and went very thoughtfully towards home.

CHAPTER IX.

'AM I in love with her?'

There comes a time when a man suddenly wakes with a start to ask himself that question, and it is one to which it is often difficult to give a clear and precise answer. There are so many shades and gradations in liking, interest and love, that it is barely possible now and then to trace where one merges into another. Graham sat over his study fire after his solitary dinner, and his mind involuntarily turned to face this question. He had been drawn from the beginning by a very strong attraction to Gwen. Of that he had no doubt whatever, but at first he was sure compassion had more than anything else —more even than admiration for her looks—to do with that feeling than any more passionate or vehement emotion. The deep and brooding sadness of her eyes, the wistful and pathetic lines of her features, had troubled first, and then engrossed his thoughts. He had fancied, in certain moods at first, that Ettie's bright, vivacious prettiness, her girlish, audacious gaiety had suited him best. She was a veritable allegra, and he had always liked bright, cheerful and pretty things. Yet, oddly enough, he had no doubt now in determining that Ettie's vivacity had ceased to fascinate, and that Gwen's reserve, even her coldness, her quiet sadness, sometimes brightened by a gleam which showed a brief revelation of what happiness might have made her, were far more alluring to his imagination, and more appealing to his heart. Ettie was shallow; a mere bright, little brook, that showed every glittering, worthless pebble that lay under its few inches, soon fathomed, soon exhausted. The elements of secrecy, of unexplored depth, of a puzzle that had to be solved, were all wanting. There was plenty of scope for fancy in studying Gwen. Besides, he was sure that in spite of fate, of the crippling narrowing grip that poverty and adverse circumstances had laid upon her, there remained underneath a tender, loyal and passionate nature. He had seen brief glimpses of it, in moments of expansion, in her ways with her mother and her little sister, both of whom Ettie either ignored or snubbed. It was Gwen who was always called upon in that household to give up and to serve. She seemed to have no reluctance, no sense of grievance in calmly accepting this *rôle*. Ettie, the father's pet and admiration, though the younger sister, quietly annexed the most comfortable chair, the crustiest bit of the loaf, the nicest portion of everything, the gaiety that was only available for one. Gwen acquiesced in this division of things, not only without grudging but apparently from choice. Madge sometimes railed at it, *she* never did. And surely there were possibilities, sleeping but to be awakened, of womanly love and passion in the depths of those pathetic, unfathomed eyes! When Graham thought of the joy of

A Girl's Past. 203

seeing them aroused, *and by him*, the triumph and satisfaction of heart if the dormant spirit in them leapt out to meet him, and owned him its master, he started to his feet in a kind of momentary transport. Surely it might be! Surely he could win her to him, shrink as she would! But why did she shrink? What made her draw back so evidently, so persistently, just as the moment seemed near, just as he was ready to seize it? What barrier, what fanciful, foolish pride, what sensitive distrust of him or of herself always came between and kept him at arm's length?

Something, impalpable as a cobweb, but stronger than his will, stretched between them. Well, he was an obstinate fellow. His will was strong, his heart firm, he was not used to take rebuffs, he could conquer a weak girl like Gwen! For, after all, she *was* weak. She was easily swayed, easily daunted. She thought a great deal of others, she had very little confidence in herself. He was often half irritated, half charmed by her genuine humility, by the entire absence of vanity and conceit in her nature, so curiously a contrast in this respect, as in every other, to her sister, whose robust good opinion of herself was evident in every bold, confident smile, in every assured glance, in every turn of the head and movement of the figure. He would convince Gwen first that she was dear and sweet to him, that he found her beautiful and desirable. He would make her believe in herself, and then in him. Bit by bit he would break down the barriers of her reserve and timidity, would first make her his friend—his dear, true, intimate friend—would not scare her by lover's talk or looks, then the rest would follow by easy, delightful steps, till her heart yielded itself to him, the hands to his hands, the lips to his lips. Ah, he had pretty well answered his own question by this time. As he reached this point, and the seductive vision he had raised took possession of him, as he imagined to himself the soft, frightened pressure of Gwen's first shy kiss, he trembled and grew hot with sudden passion. Oh, yes, he loved her! He loved her, but he would be careful and prudent. He would not hurry matters—common sense began to talk down the impulse of the moment—he would take time, would see his way.

'There are many objections,' said common sense, in that calm, unpleasant way it has sometimes. 'You don't like the family or connections. Mr Lane will not be a father-in-law to be proud of. In marrying her you would marry poverty and social inferiority. *You*, the well-to-do young country squire who has a right to look out for so very different a connection.'

'What hateful worldliness!' cried Graham's other self, the passionate and impetuous one. 'I should marry *her*, not her family, and she is a darling, fit for any man. I want a wife I can love, not a wife to bring me money or position.'

'Well, don't be in a hurry at any rate,' urged common sense, yielding ground a little. 'That would only scare her and do harm. Take your time, get to know her better, win her confidence — you haven't that yet. See how she shrank away directly you spoke of *more than friendship*.'

So far he owned common sense was in the right; instinct told him to wait, to hurry nothing. He had known her such a short time. He had promised to go home—that is to say to his mother's home—shortly, and to spend Christmas there. Nothing definite should be said or done till he returned to Erdley, perhaps till spring. He was not afraid of his own constancy nor of Gwen's changing. She was not pursued by any admirers. She stood aloof, and none but he seemed to care to get nearer to her. He did not want to rush into any hasty action. There was a charm to him in the anticipation of the slow, subtle nearing of the realisation of his hope. The generous as well as the selfish desires of Graham's nature were enlisted in the pursuit of Gwen. Poor child! She had so little, she was unhappy, she had always been unhappy. The remembrance of those few sad words of reminiscence, spoken in that pathetic voice of hers, thrilled him with pitying tenderness and with a longing to set it all right. She was so pale. Her eyes and mouth had such a weary yet patient look in them, her days were full of the hard tasks of poverty, she had neither rest nor pleasure. Even little things were against her; and, though it seemed trivial, it hurt him to notice how shabby her poor little boots were, how rusty and well-mended her gloves. She had no pretty warm wraps and furs to fence her from the increasing cold. She was still wearing her summer dress, with only a thin jacket, and she often looked pinched. Why, even to see her prettily, luxuriously clothed would be a delight! To spend money on her—choosing just what his close, keen notice showed him she wanted most—to hear her remonstrating with him on being over-generous! Oh, if she would but let him, how he would change all her life, would warm and cheer and comfort her half-starved heart!

He began to plan delightful surprises for her — little secret devices to cheat her into brightness. He would make her happy through her devotion to her mother and to little Madge. He would be liberal to the others, but these were the ones he should care to be really good to — that he would be fond of for Gwen's sake. Madge would be so happy to find herself his little sister. Graham was in a glow of impetuous feeling. His mind leapt forward into the future, and he saw it all filled with rose-coloured light. Gwen was only twenty. What if those few years of childhood and girlish life had all been dreary? there was time enough for a whole age of happiness. He was glad to remember how young she was, after all. There was not much time lost. He had always meant to win a girl's first love, first dreams, first kisses. She was so quiet, reserved and distant with men —he should be the very first. He had always loved that idea. He had a great objection to following a whole host of lovers in a girl's well-used heart. He had often told Kitty, with brotherly frankness, that he should not care for succession in a long line of flirtations, which was all any admirer of hers could boast. Kitty had been a gay, reckless, little flirt ever since she was seventeen—had never been to a dance without a desperate 'affair'; had been half engaged a dozen times, and whole engaged twice. But his Gwen had never been gay—could never have flirted. Why, if he came near her, if he only wanted to touch her hand, she shrank away with adorable timidity that was not coldness, for he could see in the troubled depth of her eyes that she was not indifferent. He hoped his mother and Kitty would understand and be good to her, but if they were not he could bear it quite well. He could imagine his dear, good, Philistine little mother pursing up her lips and putting on her worldly-wise manner. 'Oh, my dearest boy! you really *might* have done better.' He seemed to hear her voice saying the words in her emphasising fashion. 'Only a poor clergyman's daughter, and rather a shabby specimen of a clergyman, too. A girl without a penny — with *no* position *whatever*.' Then Kitty's frank detraction — Miss Kitty never minced matters, and did not at all mind being uncomplimentary— 'Well, she is pretty, but she has nothing to say for herself. She has no go in her. She is horribly reserved.'

These things should not vex him. He always got his way in the end, and he could, at any rate, manage his mother. He was perfectly independent. What people said or thought could not hurt him. They might be nasty to Gwen before she was his wife, but people must be civil to Mrs Brooke-Graham of Erdley; and when she was known, when prosperity and tenderness had made her blossom out into a subdued kind of brilliancy, which he was able to imagine for her, she would be valued and loved by those who were capable of understanding her—she would be so happy she would not need a great many friends. His visions had reached this height, he was in a glow of hope that almost seemed certainty, when it grew late, and all the village slept.

CHAPTER X.

MEANWHILE Gwen had hurried from the church to the Vicarage, and had found the family assembled there in one of its most depressing conditions. Many trifles combined had put Mr Lane into his worst humour; everything and anything served as a lighted match to the tinder of his wrath. An untidy litter of tea covered the table. Cups that had been used stood forlornly about amidst the wrecks of bread-and-butter and stale cake. A little remnant of flat, cold tea was vainly protected by a rakish-looking old tea cosy, which by no means deserved its name. Ettie, who always made herself as comfortable as circumstances allowed, had left the uninviting tea-table, and was taking up nearly the whole of the small fire, with a ragged sixpenny novel in her hand; Mr Lane fidgetted and raved about the room; his wife still sat limp, dejected and unmoving by the tray, keeping the meal as eatable as she could for the unpunctual Gwen; one pupil, the incorrigible Johnstone, was not to be seen; poor 'Topsy Turvey' leant his elbows on the table amid a perfect wreckage of spilt tea and bits of soppy bread-and-butter. His stupid, good-natured face looked calmly on as Mr Lane stormed more or less at everything. He turned, with a new access of petulance, on his elder daughter as she slipped in and took a seat by her mother.

'Late as usual! You can never have the common politeness to conform to the hours of meals. It is really too bad that one's daughter should show so little consideration for my comfort.'

'Come, papa, we did not wait for her,' murmured the mother, as Gwen sat silent. 'You had your tea at the usual time. It is Gwen who gets it cold and uncomfortable.'

'Wait! Would you have me wait? A pretty life I should lead if I gave in to all their vagaries. Cold! People deserve cold tea who can't be punctual. Upon my word it's enough to drive one crazy the way these young people go on. Where have you been?' he snapped, turning on Gwen almost savagely. 'That young scoundrel Johnstone came in, as usual, with some cock-and-bull story about you and Mr Brooke-Graham. I sent him to bed, but I really should like to know the rights of the story.'

'He was—was rude to me,' Gwen murmured, through half-closed lips, the slow, painful colour (it was always painful to her to blush) rising in her pale face. 'He followed me. I—I went into the plantation to get away from him.'

She paused suddenly, and drew a long, hard breath. Ettie watched her sharply, unsympathetically, from her place by the fire.

'What then?' demanded the father. 'Was there a row between Graham and that wretched lad?'

'He—came—up,' Gwen answered, with difficulty, pausing between each word. 'He—sent him out of the wilderness.'

'Well, what did you do then? Stop in the wilderness to be sympathised with?'

There was a sneer on his face and in his voice.

'I went to the church to practise the chants,' she answered briefly, without looking at her father.

'Yes, and someone said Mr Brooke-Graham went in too. Was that so?'

'Yes,' Gwen said, stung to sudden anger, fixing her eyes on him. 'What then?'

'What then? Why—why it was not at all a correct thing to do, not at all. You'll have the village talking about you. Your own good taste, your own delicacy, should have told you.'

'Hush, hush, papa,' Mrs Lane murmured, distressed for her child, but daring hardly to interpose in 'one of papa's moods.'

'Hold your tongue, mother,' he retorted rudely. 'I have a right to speak to Gweneth, I suppose, though I never found it did much good. You have always spoilt her, but I tell you no good ever came, or ever will come, of her secretive, underhand ways.'

The angry flush of acute pain deepened on Gwen's face. She pressed her lips together and sat still. What was the use of speaking? In such a mood, reason alike and appeal to feeling would be wasted on the violent man, in whose mind a variety of vexations small and great were pricking him to fury. Topsy Turvey made a sudden, if not agreeable, diversion. Violence of manner frightened his poor, weak soul; when he was frightened he writhed and contorted his bony frame for relief. Kicking out one nervous leg he gave a mighty jerk, which upset Gwen's cup of tea on the cloth. Mr Lane did not actually swear—in words. To that extent he managed to keep up his clerical reputation, but he raved in a tone that conveyed the idea of swearing, and poor Turvey poured out a flood of incoherent apology, ending up with a weak giggle and an attempted consolation that it was 'nearly clean cloth day.' Ettie broke into a short laugh at this, and remarked it was Thursday, she did not know how he made that out, and

Gwen escaped in the confusion. There was no fire in the drawing-room, but she preferred peace to warmth. Here was the friendly piano; she could, perhaps, forget herself in music. While she played her mother came in softly. She stood behind her, and touched her with half-timid but caressing little pats. She made hesitating beginnings at speech, which became easier to her when the girl half turned on the stool and leant back against her.

'Gwennie, dear, you must not take what papa says to heart. He has a great deal to vex him. This dreadful Johnstone boy, and poor Turvey is trying, too, one must confess. When he is irritated he says more than he really means.'

'Don't fret about it, mother dear,

don't worry about me,' Gwen's low voice said tenderly. 'I am used, you know, to his thinking badly of me. I daresay I deserve he should. I know I don't deserve that you should be unhappy about me.'

'He seems, somehow, rather annoyed with Mr Brooke-Graham. He fancied— I never did myself—that—that he liked —*Ettie*.' She paused, then added nervously: 'Of course it would be a very nice thing for her.'

Gwen said nothing, the mother went on again.

'It is foolish, I think, to imagine every man who is kind and friendly should mean — should mean — *anything*. Ettie is very young. I hope she may marry tolerably, but I don't look high for her. Gwennie, dear, what made Mr

Graham go into the church with you? Someone told papa as he came in.'

'Oh, I don't know, how should I?' Gwen cried, suddenly twisting herself from her mother. 'It was a whim, a fancy, he said it seemed peaceful. Could I make a fuss and tell him not to come?'

There was a pause, then the mother said, in a low, frightened, faltering voice,—

'You are *careful*, dear. There is—nothing?'

'Nothing, nothing,' Gwen said, vehemently. 'It is cruel, hateful to think so! Can't he even be friendly—kind—to me as he is to Ettie and Madge. Am I to have no friends at all? Am I a pariah?'

It was not often Gwen spoke so, not

often passion of any sort was allowed to get the upper hand of her. The timid mother was silenced at once. She was one of those who seek peace in 'letting things be,' but, alas, she seldom found what she sought. She hastily kissed her daughter, murmuring some soothing commonplace, and left her. Things were too difficult for her to begin combatting them. Possibly 'it would all come right in the end.' She often used this formula, which meant but little to her after the many disappointments of her troubled life. In one respect she had a well-founded confidence in a change for the better. Mr Lane's bad tempers did not generally rage very long. By supper-time he would probably have grumbled and stormed himself into a fairly quiescent state, and his usual glass of spirits and water would help to produce a milder frame of mind. Yet, though this was so, he retained a resentful, cold manner to Gwen. What business had she to be making extra bother with those plagues of pupils? It was bad enough as it was, endeavouring to keep Johnstone in decent bounds so that he could continue to receive, if not to earn, the handsome sum his sorely tried father was ready to pay to put his prodigal son out of his sight.

'What's to be done?' he growled at Gwen, in the middle of supper. 'Have I got to make his apologies? I daresay you thought too much of a drunken lad's foolishness.'

'I will speak to him myself,' Gwen said, with a sudden proud flash of scorn and anger. 'He shall beg my pardon. I won't submit to be insulted by him.'

'He didn't probably know what he was saying. You might have managed to keep it quiet, and not bring other people in.'

'I could not help,' she returned, with a proud but quivering lip. 'Mr Brooke-Graham happened to hear. He is too much of a gentleman to let a lady—a girl—be treated like that.'

'Quite a romantic adventure,' Ettie said sneeringly. 'Gwen always liked romance!'

'There was something meaning, almost viciously meaning in her voice and the quick, sharp glance which accompanied it. Gwen met both with a kind of desperate contempt, yet it was plain the little poisoned dart went

A Girl's Past. 227

home. She was very white, and her under lip trembled.

'It is difficult enough to manage such a position as is thrust upon me,' Mr Lane went on resentfully, 'to make both ends meet as best I can, with the help of what I get from these wretched boys, without complications. I should have thought you girls could keep out of their way, and manage to make things less, rather than more, difficult. No man was ever harassed and hampered as I am.'

'The girls do what they can to help, papa,' Mrs Lane said, in her sad, meek voice.

'Do they?' he returned grimly, 'I wish I could see it.'

'Let me leave home, let me take a situation somewhere,' Gwen said suddenly and breathlessly. 'I would be glad.'

'What could you do?' he asked bitterly.

'I don't know. It is not my fault that I am not educated enough for a governess, but I can sew, I can do housework. I don't mind what it is; and I have my music.'

'It would hardly help me, a clergyman, who have a position to keep up, to have a daughter in service. We must rub on, I suppose, but I do think you might manage not to make more bother with the pupils.'

Gwen forebore to answer the angry unreasonableness of her father. In truth, he hardly cared what accusation he brought against her. He could not openly state the head and front of her offending, which was simply that *she*, and not Ettie, had been placed in the position which he only vaguely guessed at. The bare idea that Gwen, rather than Ettie, might attract the squire, suggested complications and unpleasantness which, with that facile nature of his, that invariably shirked emergencies and disagreeables as long as possible, he chose not to entertain definitely, but which vaguely perplexed and irritated him. He began to consider ways and means of sending Gwen away, and bringing Ettie more and more forward, but he had not the energy of purpose either to plan or to carry out any distinct projects. He only uneasily asked his wife, when they were alone, if she had ever noticed any sort of interest in Mr Brooke-Graham's manner towards Gwen.

'It might be very awkward and unfortunate,' he added, avoiding more detail.

'No,' his wife said dubiously, 'he likes her—they are friendly. I don't think that he cares particularly for— for either of the girls, you know; I never saw much in his manner with Ettie.'

'Pooh, you never see things! He certainly admired—was taken with Ettie. I believe you might have done something in throwing them together. She is just the pretty, lively, taking girl, to attract a quiet fellow like that, and she's much prettier than Gwen.'

'I know *you* think so,' the mother could not help saying in a futile kind of championship, 'but everybody does not. There are people who call Gwen lovely!'

A Girl's Past.

'I am sorry to hear it, if they are of any use,' Mr Lane said drily. 'If you had more sense, you would wish to see Ettie well married.'

'I do—of course I do—but she is so young.'

'That is a charm in itself, a bright, girlish kittenish, young thing, pretty and full of life, she is more attractive now than she will be when she is older. I don't want Gwen to spoil her chances.'

Mrs Lane only sighed, taking refuge in silence. Life was too much for her feeble powers of pilotage; she must drift and let the children drift, sadly and vaguely, on a shifting and dangerous sea. Luck had always been against her and she feared Gwen, in inheriting her looks and many of her ways, had also come in for the same melancholy heritage of disaster. She had always been an 'unlucky child.' They must go on drifting; there was always a possibility of help.

Gwen certainly inherited much from her mother, physically and mentally, but she had a certain reserve of strength, courage and will power, which the older, weaker woman lacked; with much inconsistency, and even weakness, Gwen had some stronger qualities. She found Johnstone alone in the so-called 'study,' next morning, resting his hot, aching head on a big dictionary, and calmly demanded an apology from him, and promise of amendment. He looked up at her with feeble penitence, being in the forlorn and shivering stage of reaction — her stern, pale young face set into severe lines was as an accusing angel's to him. He feebly admired, and was weakly 'spoony' on Gwen.

'What did I do? I was rather *on*, you know, and really don't remember, Miss Lane—'

'You are always *on*,' she returned with supreme scorn, 'but anyhow, whatever state you are in, you are never to dare again to be impertinent to me!'

'I'm sure I beg your pardon if I was rude,' he said spluttering, half inclined to weep. 'I am a miserable beggar, I know. I wish I were in my coffin—I do feel so wretched.'

'You *will* die if you go on like this. No wonder you are wretched. Oh!' she cried, suddenly softening into pity in spite of her disgust, '*why* don't you stop? Why will you destroy yourself? Why don't you give it up?'

He was fairly blubbering now.

'Oh, Miss Lane, if only I could! Every morning when I wake with a devil of a headache, feeling so sick and bad, I could cut my throat; I say I never will have another drop, and I mean it at the time, but I can't go on with it—I can't. At dinner there's beer going—it picks me up, and water seems so nasty, then I want something stronger, there's every chance of getting it; why, even Mr Lane takes whisky, you know, though, of course, not too much, so I begin nipping, then I have to go on. It's in my blood. I really can't help myself.'

Gwen felt with a sudden pang that his plea had something in it. *This* was not the house, her father was not the man for the wretched boy to have a fair chance of reform. She could not truly say she had never seen her father the worse for what he had taken, though it was seldom he actually exceeded. He took such pupils, not honestly desiring their redemption, but to eke out his own slender means. A sense of degradation, of shame, hung over her. Alas! she could feel no pride in her family. Theirs was not the honest poverty which has nothing to be ashamed of.

'I wish I could help you—I am sorry for you,' she said, drawing a long, heavy sigh. 'My father ought to try and prevent you more than he does. You should not be allowed any chance at all. You are throwing your life away. Surely, surely you might draw back before it is too late.'

'It's very good of you to care—to take any trouble about me—after I was so beastly to you. What did I do, Miss Gwen? I've only the haziest notion. Was Mr Brooke-Graham there?—what happened? I know he despises me awf'ly.'

'It doesn't matter about repeating the stupid, rude things you said,' Gwen said quickly, flushing a little. 'Yes, Mr Graham was very angry. Don't let's talk about it. If it never happens again, *never* mind,' with gathering severity, 'whether you are "on" or not, I will not say any more about it.'

'You'll forgive me? You'll not hate me?'

'I'll *forgive* you,' Gwen said slowly, 'but as to the rest—if you saw what you were like sometimes—'

'You can't help hating me?'

'Not *hating*, but nobody, however kind, could help *despising* you. You are so young—you might be different, surely you might. Won't you try again?'

Her deep, rich, sad voice was full of pleading pathos, her great eyes full of sad entreaty. Johnstone groaned.

'It's no use saying I will. I've no faith left in myself,' he muttered drearily, passing his hot, trembling hand through his uncombed hair. 'It's too strong for me—the temptation, I mean—it's in my blood. It's all very well for a girl like you to talk, who doesn't know what temptation means, or badness—'

Gwen made a sudden movement. She seemed to shrink from his words with a motion of denial. 'I do know,' she said hoarsely, under her breath. 'I'm not good. Oh, I *am* sorry for you!'

'God bless you for that,' he spluttered out sobbingly, and suddenly stretching out that hot, sodden hand of his to touch hers. With all her repugnance for him, Gwen let him hold her cold little fingers a moment, but when, from clasping he proceeded to try and kiss them, she snatched her hand away and left the room suddenly. The poor boy, who had lost the wholesome self-restraint and bashfulness of youth, wiped his eyes without any fresh sense of shame at his own passing emotion. No regret was strong enough to overcome the low desires of his poor, tainted, limited soul.

CHAPTER XI.

AFTER the conclusion Graham had arrived at, as to the state of his feelings towards Gwen, he naturally desired and sought for every opportunity of seeing her. But he was oddly baffled. Gwen seemed to have gone back to the first habits of her life at Erdley. She was busy at home or in the village; she did not pay visits, and it was always Ettie and not she who took part in any small festivity. When they met by chance, she was brief, cold, reserved, her eyes would not meet his, she would not be drawn into any but the very briefest conversations. Mr Lane was always to be seen, ready to button-hole the young squire, was expansive, endlessly talkative. Ettie was easily to be met, and ready to be responsive, a little coquettish, as alluring as she knew how to be. But Gwen had drawn back into the shadows. She was quiet, repellent, uncommunicative. Without making a *confidante* of her, Graham had allowed his friend Mrs Willoughby, with whom he was on very intimate terms, to know that he was interested in the eldest Miss Lane, He was the more confidential because the Willoughbys themselves liked and admired Gwen, and the kind lady did her utmost to form a friendship with the shy, silent girl, to induce her to come often to see her, and to try and gain her confidence.

Graham was given as many opportunities as Mrs Willoughby could manage for seeing Gwen at her house, but they were few enough. He seemed to gain no ground. The very difficulty of approach, her very backwardness, however, had charms for this obstinate young fellow, who loved to set his will against an obstacle. In his eyes, Gwen's very reserve was a potent attraction, and her sister's forwardness disgusted and alienated him.

Christmas was not far off. He should have to leave Erdley without having gained a step. But there was time enough, he thought; he had no fear of rivalry. Gwen was not popular with the youth of the neighbourhood, even though her beauty of face and voice were acknowledged. Ettie, though often laughed at and treated with scant respect, had won far more notice and admiration. When he came back, when spring with its sweetness of life and promise of joy was with them, he would win her yet.

He was very constant in calling on Mrs Willoughby, and always contrived to bring the conversation ingeniously round to parish questions, which were likely to introduce the *locum tenens* and his family. Mrs Willoughby, though never uncharitable or censorious, was not a woman who liked or approved of everybody; and she let it be perceived, though she avoided strong speech, that Mr Lane was not one of her favourites, nor was his younger daughter. Mrs Lane she tolerated with half contemptuous pity. The neat, precise Mrs Willoughby, who had brought the dainty carefulness of her old maidenly years into her married home, could not help considering the clergyman's wife 'shiftless,' and weakly indulgent towards a state of affairs in her house which no mistress should allow. But she was a 'gentle, kind soul,' Mrs Willoughby admitted, 'and no doubt has had a great deal to put up with.'

'Ay,' Graham replied with conviction, 'it needs a strong angel not to be the worse for poverty. Mrs Lane has been over-weighted in life, poor thing. No one, with the least chivalry in him should condemn her.'

'I hope I condemn no one,' Mrs Willoughby said, in her sweet, precise voice. 'I daresay there are excuses even for *Mr* Lane; yet I can't esteem him as a man or a clergyman, outside the church. He is a good preacher.'

'Considering that, it is rather odd, isn't it, he has never got promotion?'

'There may be plenty of reasons. Surely you don't think it enough for a man to *preach* well?'

'I? I am afraid I have little opinion of parsons at the best. They always seem to be rather hybrid, indefinite creatures; I don't expect them both to preach and to practise excellence. Yet, possibly, Lane is no hypocrite. He is a facile, fluid, emotional sort of fellow. I daresay, while he is declaiming "on the side of the angels" he feels what he says—but the world, the flesh and the devil waiting outside the church doors, are too strong for him. He is not, however, unkind to the poor people. They seem rather to like him.'

'Oh, I believe he is good-natured, in a way. But Miss Lane—Gwen, 'as they call her—is the best in parish work. The old folks speak highly of her, she goes in and sits with them, reads, and sometimes sings. Old Betty Harris told me she asked her to sing her a hymn, as "she'd heard tell of her wonderful voice and couldn't get to church to listen to it," and Gwen sang "like a nightingale," the old body said, "Lead, kindly light," and "Hark! hark! my soul."'

'That was very kind,' Graham said fervently, his eyes shining and a tender sort of smile on his lips. He vowed inwardly to take old Betty a pound of tea.

'Yes, it was. Betty told me her voice sounded that sweet and sad she was fain to cry " like a babby." '

'It *is* a sad voice.'

'Very. Miss Lane has trained the choir boys very well, and they are really improued in behaviour — such troublesome monkeys as they were at first! She has a nice way with them, and is not hard on the naughtiest. Her father and the churchwardens wanted her to have Bobby Hughes expelled, he behaved so badly, but she begged him off, Mr Willoughby heard her. She is very charitable to the *mauvais sujets* of the village. That poor girl, Mary Witts, who came home in disgrace, she has befriended, I know, for her mother told me how surprised they were at the parson's young lady going to see Mary every day while she was so ill.'

'I have noticed that Gwen—that Miss Lane is particularly charitable to all the black sheep. It is singularly unlike the behaviour of most of our good Christian ladies — of course, I except *you*, Mrs Willoughby.'

'It strikes me, Graham,' Mrs Willoughby said, glancing up from her fine work with a demure smile, 'that you have noticed a great many things in Miss Lane!'

He blushed quite boyishly, with a little conscious laugh.

'Well, I own I admire her very much.'

'Yes; but admiration may mean very little, or a great deal. I suppose you think her very pretty?'

'Oh, yes, certainly! A fellow would be blind who didn't.'

'And she has a charming contralto voice, very sweet, rich and thrilling—that goes a long way.'

'No one could deny that.'

'Yes, well—but beyond these points—you don't stop at admiring her face and voice?'

'No, I don't,' Graham declared stoutly.

'She is not — not *clever*, not highly cultivated?'

'Perhaps not exactly, but there is plenty of thought in her; she does not talk much, but she reads a great deal. I daresay people would not consider her *clever*.'

'But good—you are sure of her goodness, though she has not been trained in the best of schools?'

A Girl's Past. 249

'What does that comprehensive word *good* imply to you, Mrs Willoughby? Not perfect. I don't consider her perfect nor *goody*, but when you say *good* you mean—'

'True, upright, conscientious. We don't know very much, do we, about her? She *may* be all these, as we see she is kind and charitable; but are you sure she is?'

'Oh, I am sure she is *true*, perfectly true and pure!' Graham cried with a sudden enthusiasm, carried beyond the careful level of conventional speech. 'Look in her face—'

Mrs Willoughby gently shook her head, saying, in mild remonstrance,— 'Graham! Graham! you men are all alike. You see a pretty face, and you give the owner of it credit for every virtue under the sun. Don't be run away with by your eyes, my dear boy. Forgive my saying just this one bit of middle-aged prudence: be quite sure you are doing wisely for yourself and all belonging to you, before you really and definitely give away your heart.'

'I'm not just like other men,' Graham declared sturdily. 'I've seen plenty of pretty girls—heaps of them, here in England and in different parts of the world. Beauty alone doesn't appeal to me; many a lovely face has left me as cold as a stone. But there's a fate in these things—magnetism or what you like. Why is it that some people draw one's heart to them? One can't say, but it is so.'

'When you are young and romantic,'

A Girl's Past.   251

Mrs Willoughby said with a little sigh, perhaps, for her lost youth.

'My dear Mrs Willoughby! you are as romantic as any one. Don't pretend to have forgotten how to be. Look here!' He lifted up the book that lay beside her, 'The most *lovery* of novels! But you seemed interested in it. Don't throw cold water on my sentiments after that.'

'I don't, Graham. I believe in *love*, but I believe in common sense in marriages.'

'Well. I'm not married, nor engaged yet. When I am, you shall say what you like.'

'What do you think about Graham and Miss Lane?' Mrs Willoughby asked her husband rather anxiously after this talk. 'Is it a serious thing, do you suppose?'

Mr Willoughby shrugged his lean shoulders and fidgeted his long hands and feet as he was wont to do when perplexed.

'How can I say, my dear? Women are more acute than men in reading the weather signs of love. He stares at her a vast deal in church, and he is very regular there—both are suspicious symptoms. And she looks conscious, particularly shy, and she avoids him—so much I *have* noticed; but to distinguish between a passing fit and a chronic disease of love, is beyond my diagnosis.'

'Yes! I've thought too, lately, that she avoids him,' Mrs Willoughby said doubtfully. 'I wonder what that means. It would be a splendid thing for her!'

'If she happens to like him,' Mr Willoughby remarked drily.

'To like him! Everybody must like Graham.'

'Well, love, then. I suppose all women don't *love* him; that would be awkward. Perhaps Miss Lane is not so worldly as you give her credit for being—'

'But I do believe she likes Graham and I am sure Mr and Mrs Lane would be delighted.'

'Oh, they would adore him, as a son-in-law; of that there is no shadow of doubt, no possible doubt whatever. But would Graham reciprocate? Would he find Mr Lane a satisfactory *beau père*? There are more doubts on that point. I don't think it is exactly an ideal family to marry into.'

'Nor I. But I like Gwen, in spite of her quiet, reserved ways. She is so pathetic; she appeals first to one's compassion, then affection.'

'I like her too — a hundred times better than that pert, forward, third-rate miss, her sister. I long to box her ears when she flourishes about and laughs—ye gods, how the child laughs at nothing!'

'I do not approve of Miss Ettie Lane at all,' Mrs Willoughby said in her most precise tone. 'Still, there is no likeness between the sisters. No one can call the elder girl a flirt or forward, she is too backward. Her eyes have a way of going to one's heart, somehow, and her voice—it is the most *larmoyant* voice I ever heard—when she sang at that village concert, I found myself actually crying.'

A Girl's Past.

'I suppose her eyes and her voice have got at Brooke-Graham's heart, too. Well, time will show if there is anything to come of this or not. I shall continue to think it would be a misfortune for him to marry into the Lane family. People are beginning to gossip finely about the parson. One discounts half of what the Willards and the Barnetts say, of course, yet there is a residuum of truth, I suppose. He certainly is getting in debt, he certainly likes a "wee drappie"; he has a foolish, incautious tongue, and his pupils are a scandal to a quiet neighbourhood. But he may be more unlucky than bad, and I believe he is. I'm sorry for that sad-faced wife of his, at any rate, for Lane certainly has a temper.'

'I hope it may not have gone deep with Graham.'

'Or that Miss Lane won't have him.'

'My dear! That *is* unlikely!'

'Why? There may be another love in the background. She has the look of a girl who has a story.'

'She is so young.'

'What? Twenty or twenty-one? Lots of time for mischief. We must wait and see what comes of it.'

END OF VOL. I.

COLSTON AND COMPANY, PRINTERS, EDINBURGH.

www.ingramcontent.com/pod-product-compliance
Lightning Source LLC
Chambersburg PA
CBHW021343230426
43666CB00006B/394